LEWES
PAST

Lewes from the top of Chapel Hill, with the *Cricketers Arms* in the foreground, *c.*1865, from a private collection.

LEWES PAST

Helen Poole

Phillimore

2000

Published by
PHILLIMORE & CO. LTD.
Shopwyke Manor Barn, Chichester, West Sussex

ISBN 1 86077 127 0

Printed and bound in Great Britain by
BIDDLES LTD.
Guildford, Surrey

Contents

List of Illustrations

Frontispiece: Lewes from the top of Chapel Hill, with the *Cricketers Arms* in the foreground, *c.*1865.

Acknowledgements

Several collectors of Lewes material have been very generous in allowing me to use their treasures and I appreciate this very much. I should also specifically like to thank the following for permission to use illustrations from their fine collections: Mr Bob Cairns for numbers 45, 65, 66, 82, 85, 106, 108, 115, 141 & 147: Mr. Tom Reeves for 38, 47 & 131, as well as the examples of his family's long recording of Lewes, now cared for by the Sussex Archaeological Society: Lewes District Council for 54: Sussex Archaeological Society for 2, 4, 7, 9, 11, 15, 23-4, 31-4, 40-1, 43-4, 48-9, 51, 56, 59-63, 67-8, 70-3, 76-7, 83, 87-8, 96, 103, 113, 117, 122-4, 127-8, 130, 132-3, 135-40, 144-6, 148-9, 151-4, 158-9, 164-73.

People have been very kind to me whilst I was writing this book. My family has graciously put up with the sight of my back for hours on end as I worked at the computer; even the cat made no real attempt to rearrange my carefully ordered piles of reference papers. I have had enormous help and encouragement from friends and from staff in all the libraries that I mention at the head of the Bibliography, but special mention must be made of the volunteers at the Library in Barbican House. Anyone with an active interest in Sussex history has cause to be grateful for the years spent bringing together an invaluable resource of reference material, from mainstream books to an amazing range of ephemera. Nothing is too much trouble in the search for that vital missing clue or illustration, no matter how obscure the requirement. I should like to record my thanks publicly to the two who very kindly put my name forward for this commission—I hope that they won't regret it!

Above all, I want to thank Mr. Richard Philcox whose knowledge of Lewes is exceptional and who has spent many hours sharing this with me, back to the days of our articles in the *Lewes Leader*. His devoted care of the excellent photographic collections of the Sussex Archaeological Society at Barbican House is unparalleled and this book would have been poorer without it. I dedicate *Lewes Past* to him as a small way of thanking him for his constant support and encouragement.

Introduction

Lewes has been an important element in the life of Sussex for over a thousand years. Its earliest history only survives in enigmatic hints but about 900 it became one of the towns designated by King Alfred and his successors to keep the Viking threat at bay. 1066 brought to Sussex William de Warenne, a Norman landowner who fought beside Duke William at the Battle of Hastings. He was rewarded for his services by the Rape of Lewes, a swathe of land from the coast to Worth Forest and the Surrey boundary, along the River Ouse, the second largest river in Sussex. From its vantage point on a promontory, Lewes Castle dominated one of the few river crossings and was ideally placed to be the focal point of this new military and administrative unit.

William de Warenne became Earl of Surrey just before his death in 1088 and was buried beside his wife Gundrada in their new foundation of the Priory of St Pancras. The family had strong links with royalty and remained loyal at the time of the most decisive day in Lewes history, 14 May 1264, when Simon de Montfort defeated the army of Henry III. As a result of this victory, negotiations began which were to result in a major step forward in democracy, the calling of the first English Parliament.

Lewes remained in the family's hands until 1347 with the death of the last male of the line, John de Warenne, 8th Earl of Surrey. Lewes passed to his nephew, the Earl of Arundel, who already had a grand Sussex castle, so the Castle's importance began to decline. De Warenne's colours, the chequy yellow and blue, are shown on the flag flown from the Castle keep and on the pub sign by the entrance to Surrey County Cricket Club's ground at the Oval. They also dominate the town's coat of arms, where they are joined by the lion rampant of the Fitzalan earls of Arundel.

Lewes has long had a reputation for being independently minded, which is appropriate in a county town of Sussex whose people 'won't be druv'. Protestantism took a strong hold, despite the presence nearby of Catholic gentry, and 41 of the 288 non-Catholics burnt in the reign of Mary Tudor were from Sussex. Seventeen of these men and women died in Lewes, starting with the indomitable Derick Carver who came to Lewes to die for his faith on 22 July 1555. He was burnt in a barrel that was set up outside the *Star* with his Bible inside: Carver retrieved it and threw it into the crowd, before exhorting the spectators to remain true to Christ's Gospel. Nonconformity survived, despite persecution particularly in the late 17th century, but anti-papal feeling remained strong and was a major theme of Lewes Bonfire celebrations.

From its strategic position overlooking the Ouse valley, Lewes held important markets and fairs, serving the surrounding countryside which was strongly agricultural. Industries also developed and the town became the centre for professional men and the gentry who built or modified town houses which still give the heart of the town an air of Georgian elegance. The firebrand Tom Paine lived in Lewes from 1768 to 1774, retaining some contact with the town after he left to take an active part in revolution in France and America. Now his name survives in a special ale produced by Harvey's of Lewes, the sole survivor of what was a lively brewing tradition. The coming of the railways caused further changes, as more recently has the influx of people connected with the two Universities of Sussex and Brighton. In 1881 Lewes achieved borough status and on 1 April 1889 the town became the headquarters of the new East Sussex County Council. This continues in a slightly truncated form and, coupled with its standing as the headquarters of Lewes District Council, brings many people and services to work in the town. Artistic life is very strong and is part of a healthy tradition which brought Rodin here in 1903 and his superb marble statue of *The Kiss* arrived a year later to a mixed reception, very different from its pulling power in 1999.

The aim of this look at Lewes past is to fill out the picture outlined in the *Victoria County History* and to give some idea of what gives this town its character. Many areas of Lewes history have been described very fully in recent years, so are not covered in detail here, but a bibliography is provided for anyone wishing to follow up any of the subjects. Otherwise, wherever possible, eyewitness accounts have been used. There is also extensive use of the words of the historians starting with Paul Dunvan in 1795 and continuing with several 19th-century sources, from the monumental works by the Rev. Thomas Walker Horsfield to guidebooks and reminiscences.

Many national figures commented on Lewes matters, from Daniel Defoe to Virginia Woolf. Where relevant, the local authors are introduced as they appear in the text, but three have been selected as examples here, as their contribution is particularly significant. First is Mark Antony Lower, who was described by E.V. Lucas as 'most interesting of Sussex archaeologists'. Lower was born in Chiddingly on 14 July 1813 and came to Lewes about 1835, establishing a school in Lancaster Street. The students in his care had an interesting education: in 1852 he recorded: 'Armed with pickaxes and shovels my pupils and I have partially excavated a barrow near the race-course', being lucky enough to find four skeletons. *The Dictionary of National Biography* said of him:

> The foundation of the Sussex Archaeological Society in 1846 was mainly due to his exertions, and it was this event which decided the course of his future career. Besides being the honorary secretary of the society and the editor of its yearly volume of collections, he engaged in a series of works, which extended his fame as an antiquary throughout the kingdom.

He lived at St Anne's House from about 1853, though he sold it in 1867, after which it was knocked down and 'replaced by a modern structure of metropolitan cut', in recent years the YMCA. Lower died on 22 March 1876 and was buried in St Anne's churchyard, leaving behind a rich legacy of well-researched and wittily phrased works on Lewes and Sussex topics.

Charles Wille was older than Lower, being born in Lewes on 29 December 1797 and dying on 18 June 1878. He earned his living as a timber merchant and the sawing shed in his yard was damaged during the dramatic avalanche in Lewes in 1836. He was involved in many of the town's activities and recorded events as diverse as problems with Bonfire Night or the arrival of the Prisoners of War from the Crimea. His diary was written for his own interest and not for a wider audience.

Much later, Mrs. Alice Dudeney was an established writer whose novels were compared favourably with those of Thomas Hardy. She was born in 1866 and lived for many years at what is now Brack Mound House. When she died in 1945, she left her diaries to the Sussex Archaeological Society, with instructions to keep them sealed for 25 years. They provide an observant, if somewhat malicious, perspective on Lewes and are in tune with her statement that 'it is not the affair of a novelist to whitewash humanity'.

The sources quoted all have their own agenda but they are an invaluable resource in helping us to see what makes Lewes the town that it is. William Cobbett called it 'a model of solidity and neatness', while Pevsner felt that 'its character as a county town is unmistakable. It lies proudly and picturesquely on a hill, dominated ... by its castle'.

I hope that the words and pictures that follow will help everyone to reach their own conclusions and ideally to share my enthusiasm for a very special place.

29.2.2000   HELEN POOLE

One

Lewes Landmarks

E.V. Lucas wrote of Lewes in 1904:

> Apart from the circumstance that the curiosities collected by the county's Archaeological Society are preserved in the castle, Lewes is the museum of Sussex; for she has managed to compress into small compass more objects of antiquarian interest than any town I know.

He did not have to ignore some of the unattractive public buildings of the 20th century, but otherwise his statement bears repetition nearly 100 years later.

The first matter to establish in connection with Lewes is the meaning of the place name. The general view is that the word derives from *hlaewas*, meaning hills or mounds, perhaps from the Brittonic word for hillsides. Modern research suggests that it could take its name from the number of artificial mounds or tumuli in the area, giving force to the theory that Lewes was occupied before its traditional starting point of 900.

Lewes is essentially a gap town, built on a chalk promontory which is exposed behind Cliffe. It commands a narrow crossing of the river Ouse, which curves round the north and the east, while the Winterbourne acts as a border to the south. Only the west needs man-made defences, of which traces of the earthworks survive. Anyone who has seen the impact of recent heavy rains knows that the Ouse is capable of extensive flooding and, in common with much of the coastal strip, the land to the south of the Priory can be marshy. These marshes or brooks were gradually brought under control for farming, long after the successful cultivation on the Downs, where ancient lynchets can still be seen. These traces of one-way ploughing have given their name to the houses built in 1951 at the foot of Malling Down.

Though there are many casual finds from prehistoric times or the Roman period, no

1 South-east view of Lewes by C.J. Greenwood, after the arrival of the railway, seen on the left.

2 St John sub Castro by Henry Petrie, *c.*1803/4, showing the original church with its blocked Saxon doorway and the monument to Magnus.

recognisable settlement pattern has emerged. Neolithic long barrows have been found in the area, as at Cliffe Hill. There is other evidence of prehistoric occupation in that area, particularly on the Malling-Caburn block of downland, where recent fieldwork located more early sites from the Late Neolithic/Early Bronze Age period. The prehistoric ridgeway is close to the town, as are Roman routes, one of which was traced by Ivan Margary from London to Malling Hill. Caburn and Ranscombe to the south-east of Lewes and Saxonbury to the south-west show signs that the neighbouring hills were used by farmers, to some extent for defence. Roman burials have been found in

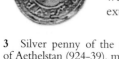

3 Silver penny of the reign of Aethelstan (924-39), minted in Lewes by Wilebald.

Lewes, including one in the castle mound. Lower wrote in 1870: 'The church-yard of St John occupies part of a very small camp considered to be Roman, part of the *vallum* of which is traceable.' The *Victoria County History* agrees that this earthwork may be the site of the earliest settlement of Lewes, but other evidence of pre-Saxon times is not conclusive.

From about 900 records become more helpful as Lewes was recorded in the Burghal Hidage. This records the systematic fortifications throughout Southern England against the Danes from the reign of Edward the Elder, possibly recording an earlier defence set up by King Alfred. The Burghal Hidage worked on the principle that a specified area of land was allotted to each stronghold, so that if one man was sent in time of need from each hide, each part of the defences could be defended by four men. It names 30 centres, of which four are in Sussex, and records Lewes with 1,300 hides, which suggested a wall 5,363 feet long. So far, excavations have not located definite Saxon fortifications, which may lie under the later medieval walls.

The threat from Danish Vikings gradually faded and Lewes prospered. King Aethelstan, son of Edward, tried to standardise currency throughout England and set up mints in several towns which had achieved some commercial importance. Lewes had two while Hastings and Chichester had one each and continued to produce silver coinage under the Norman rulers. Names of the minters in Lewes are known, starting with Wilebald in Aethelstan's reign. The longest survivor was Oswold who minted in Lewes from the reign of Aethelred to that of William I. Wulwine the moneyer owed 79s. 2d. in 1168, 'but he cannot be found'.

In 1066 other Vikings came from Normandy and conquered England at Hastings. Sussex was carved up originally into five rapes, of which the Rape of Lewes was the central one. At this time Lewes was valued at £26 a year and its population was estimated at 1,500-2,000. Saxo-Norman pottery has been found in six sites in the town, along the central ridge and the northern part of what is thought to be the old burh round St John sub Castro. Before 1066 'their custom was, if the King wished to send his men in his absence to guard the sea, they collected 20s. from all men whosesoever the land was, and those who had charge of arms in the shops had these.'

By 1086 Domesday Book records Lewes as a borough, valued at £34 a year, raised from fixed rents and issues, with a reeve to collect the fines. Anyone selling a horse in the borough paid the reeve a penny, for an ox ½d., and

> for a man 4d., wherever he buys within the Rape. Whoever sheds blood is fined 7s. 4d. A man who commits adultery or rape is fined 8s. 4d., and a woman as much. The King has the adulterous man, the Archbishop the woman.

Confusingly the entry on Lewes Castle occurs with William de Warenne's possessions in Norfolk but there are other intriguing references in the

4 The keep of Lewes Castle, with St Michael's church tower on the left, before 1939. Photographed by E.J. Bedford.

Sussex survey, as at Southease where the entry includes 'from the villagers 38,500 herrings; for porpoises £4'. Excavations at Lewes Priory produced porpoise bones, presumably caught in the Channel to supplement land-based foods.

The medieval plan of the central part of Lewes survives, with tightly packed houses still overshadowed from most viewpoints by the castle. After the Battle of Hastings William I rewarded William de Warenne, one of his most loyal supporters, with the Rape of Lewes, though he later had to exchange parts of it with neighbouring rapes. He probably built his first castle after 1066 on the more easterly of the present castle's two mounds, generally known as Brack Mount, which is on a natural spur. This would have been a wooden motte and bailey, of the type seen in the Bayeux Tapestry.

The castle was soon extended by building on the nearby mound to the south-west, now the very familiar site of the shell keep, making the castle fitter to be the lord's residence. The towers were added in the 13th century and excavations in 1985-88 inside the shell keep found two phases of building with associated artefacts. Between the two mottes was a bailey or courtyard, now filled by the Bowling Green and private houses, but

then providing accommodation for the lord and his household. In 1240 repairs were carried out to the 'Old Hall and Chamber within the Baily of the Castle of Lewes'.

Entry to this impressive stronghold was through the Norman gateway, much of which survives with its link into the curtain wall and

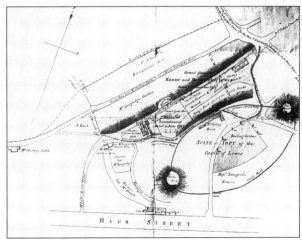

5 Plan of Lewes Castle after the building of New Road, *c*.1830.

6 Lewes Castle. The keep interior, postcard showing the two surviving towers and the tree in the centre which may be on the line of a well.

7 Lewes Castle excavation near the south wall of the keep, Easter 1985.

shows the characteristic early herringbone flint work. It was later hidden from view from the outside by the 14th-century Barbican, which with the keep has become symbolic of the town of Lewes. A deep dry moat protected the castle where necessary, but this was filled in and built on, with a school and a chapel amongst the houses. When the Sussex Archaeological Society leased the castle in 1850, they were allowed 'to pull down such of the modern buildings near the Castle Gateway as may not be required for the purposes of the Society'. This created the Gun Garden which today acts as a venue for events from the Knots of May to historic re-enactments.

When Gideon Mantell dug into the mound of the castle keep in 1814, he found that 'the natural undisturbed chalk-rock extends to the height of twelve feet above the garden, and that all above is artificial, being a compound of chalk rubble, mould, rubbish etc.' Brack Mount, too,

8 The Barbican and House of F. Frankfort Moore, Lewes. Postcard showing the Norman gateway, taken before 1924 when Moore left Castle Precincts House for St Leonards.

9 Castle Wall above Castle Ditch Lane, February 1957, photographed by Reeves.

10 Castle Gateway, Lewes, taken from the Gun Garden and showing the position of both gateways in relation to the dry moat.

11 'The Gatehouse of Lewes Castle' by James Rouse, 1825.

was built up with chalk blocks, but in both cases it is reasonable to suppose that the mounds predated the need for a castle, fitting as they do into a wider pattern of early mounds in Lewes. This would help to explain the almost unique provision of two mounds for Lewes Castle: one explanation for this is that the second mound was built because it was no longer so necessary to protect the river valley, which could be done effectively from Brack Mount, whereas the keep mound dominated the growing town more satisfactorily. Since 1813 Brack Mount has been guarded by a fascinating house on many levels, built in 1813 as a watch-tower by the London-Lewes carrier, John Shelley, and, according to Horsfield, 'the south wall of Mr. Shelley's Warehouse on Castle Banks is part of the old fortification refaced'.

William de Warenne was also responsible with his wife Gundrada for the other major Norman building in the Lewes area, the great Cluniac Priory of St Pancras at what he called 'my island of Southover'. It was founded between 1078 and 1082 as they wished 'to give a church which we had converted from wood to stone which had been of old time dedicated to St Pancras'. This soon gave way to a well-built stone church, which in its turn was replaced by the Great Church, leaving the original to be demoted to acting as the Infirmary Chapel. Lewes was the only daughter house outside France of the great Benedictine house of Cluny, which in its prime was the centre of monastic reform and of art and learning in Europe.

Gundrada died in childbirth at Castle Acre, her husband's Norfolk base, but her body was returned to Lewes Priory for burial in 1085. Three years later her husband was buried beside her. Their bodies were not allowed eternal rest, as they were put into small lead cists decades later, long after the bones were disarticulated. The magnificent memorial to Gundrada was lost at the Dissolution and was found, upside down, in Isfield Church in 1775 and brought back to Southover by Sir William Burrell. The saga does not end

12 Lewes Castle gateway showing the buildings on the left that were demolished from 1850.

13 Brack Mound House with Brack Mount in the background, 1999.

14 Ruins of the Priory, a 19th-century engraving showing the relationship between the Priory in the foreground and the town behind it.

there, as the cists were found in 1845 when the railway carved its impious way through the Priory ruins. Their bodies were measured and discovered to be about 5ft. 7in. for Gundrada and over 6ft. for her husband, and even her still born baby may have been there. The cists were reburied in a magnificent new chapel built onto St John, Southover, but the skeletons were not as complete as they should have been, as teeth were taken as mementoes. Seven are said to have gone, of which one is on display at Anne of Cleves House.

Religion was very important to our medieval forebears and occasionally spiritual help was invoked where temporal help had failed. In the 13th century the son of Hugh Bigod lay ill with his relatives at Lewes Castle. His father, unable to watch the boy's last hours, left Lewes but a lady in waiting remembered that the child had been christened by St Richard. She therefore measured his length with lint and made it into a taper which she then burned in the castle chapel, praying to the saint. Thanks to this, the boy recovered.

The major contribution that Lewes has made to the history of democracy came in May 1264 when Henry III arrived at the Priory with his troops and camp followers to celebrate the patronal festival of St Pancras on 12 May. Simon de Montfort's army prepared for the fight at Boxholt, on the high ground two miles from Lewes, near Blackcap. On 14 May he defeated the king, his brother and his eldest son, who later as Edward I became one of the best military leaders ever to hold the English throne. Seven hundred and thirty-two years later this was recreated in part by another Prince Edward, now Earl of Wessex, for his series *Crown and Country*, when the battlefield of Lewes reverberated to the sound of motor bikes.

The reality of the battle must have been horrific. A monk of Lewes recorded that in the deadly battle between the king and his barons when

> the greatest part of the king's army was utterly overthrown between prime and noon … many of the greatest men of England, who held with the king, wounded in their heads and bodies even unto death, the number of which dead is reckoned at 2,700, more or less.

The castle stood firm for the king but its garrison set fire to the town, while de Montfort's troops

15 The first Priory church with the Priory Mound behind it, photograph taken by Meads in the 1920s, before the start of the Priory's reconstruction and consolidation by Walter Godfrey and his successors at Carden & Godfrey.

besieged the priory and fired burning arrows into the church. Structural damage was small, though the soldiers were said to have defiled the altars. At length, with all the major cards in the hands of Simon de Montfort, the fighting stopped and the talking began again.

Negotiations went on all night and, thanks largely to the Franciscans in the town, a Mise or settlement was agreed between the triumphant barons and the captive royals. By the Mise of Lewes, both princes, Edward and his brother Henry, were to be hostages and a committee of arbitration was set up, with powers to draw up a final settlement. After lengthy discussions, this led to the summoning of the first parliament in 1265 and, although Simon de Montfort was defeated and killed that same year at Evesham, his groundwork survived. There are surprisingly few relics in Lewes from the battle, but the excavation at the site of St Nicholas Hospital on Western Road in 1994 found over 100 burials, two of whose skulls had deep cuts that could have been made by a weapon wielded in anger on 14 May 1264. One had begun to heal before the man died

but there is a local tradition that many of the victims of the battle were buried here.

The strain on the Priory's hospitality and the town's resources must have been enormous as they suffered from their unwilling participation in the battle. In 1266 a three-year murage grant was awarded to the townspeople of Lewes, so that they could raise tolls to repair the damage done to their town walls in 1264.

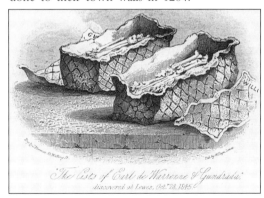

16 The cists of Earl de Warenne and Gundrada, found when the railway cutting went through the Priory ruins in October 1845.

17 The first floor of the Barbican, showing the model of the castle in the foreground and the *trompe l'oeil* paintings of weapons and shields by David Edy. The chequerboard shields in gold and blue are for the descendants of William de Warenne.

18 Engraving of 13th-century aquamanile or water jug in glazed pottery, found when digging the southern entrance to the railway tunnel under the castle and once thought to represent a knight from the Battle of Lewes, though it is more likely to be a huntsman.

A further murage grant for five years from 1334 helped with the defences and this may link in with the building of the Barbican at the Castle. This had no real defensive purpose, despite the machicolations, but it was an elegant status symbol, similar in style to a slightly later version at Carisbrooke Castle. Walwers Lane preserves the name of William le Walewere, the builder of walls, who was recorded as paying his taxes in

1296, before becoming MP for Lewes in 1319. The work on the wall by him and his predecessors is clearest in Castle Ditch Lane but there are other remains and street names such as Watergate Lane, Eastgate and Westgate are useful in preserving the traditional lines. Westgate Street car park shelters under a stretch of the town defences, not to mention the *White Lion* inn sign rescued and displayed there by the Friends of Lewes.

The line of William de Warenne's family ended in 1347 and the Earl of Arundel took over as Lord of Lewes through his wife. The Rape of Lewes proved not to be high on their list of priorities and in 1377, when the French with 40 ships attacked Rottingdean and the road open to Lewes, the only person ready to lead out a force against them was John de Caroloco, the Lewes Prior, backed by Sir John Falseley, Sir Thomas Cheyne and a squire John Brocas. They defended bravely, to the extent that the French abandoned their attempt on Lewes, but the Prior was captured and his monks were forced to pay a heavy ransom to obtain his return. In recognition of this, the Pope appropriated to Lewes Priory three churches in 1391,

> in consideration of their losses of arable and fruit-bearing lands, meadows, pasturages, etc, through maritime and other inundations, of the ransom they have had to pay for their prior, taken by the French and Spaniards near the priory, and long held captive in France, of the destruction by the same of their possessions, the burning of their crops, and the capture of their serfs, whereby the priory, in which there are at present 58 monks and one lay-brother, and which is situate near the king's highway, cannot sustain itself nor exercise hospitality.

The Poll Tax returns for Lewes in 1378 survive, listing men over the age of 15 except paupers. There are 125 names, mostly on the minimum rate of 4d., up to Henry Werkman, a buyer of wool, at 6s.8d. This argues a settled society, with two constables in post but, if this were settled, it did not last. After the Peasants' Revolt of 1381, the Rector of St Michael's Church and other local people, 'came armed to Lewes, broke his closes and his gates, doors and windows of his castle there, threw down his buildings, consumed and destroyed ten casks of wine, value £100, and burned his rolls, rentals and other muniments', according to the absentee landlord of the site, the

19 Model of the Battle of Lewes Memorial, presented to Lewes by its long-serving MP, Sir Tufton Beamish, to celebrate the 700th anniversary of the battle. It was designed by Enzo Plazzotta and now stands near the Priory.

Earl of Arundel. This Sussex magnate was seized by the enemies of his friend Richard II and executed on 21 September 1397, 'no more shrinking or changing colour than if he were going to a banquet'. The inventory of his possessions gave some idea of the air of neglect that hung round the castle, with 'various bits of old lead from roofs of buildings, found in the chapel there', and guns but no ammunition. Dissent remained and in 1450 general pardons were given for participation in Jack Cade's rebellion to a large number of named individuals in Lewes, Cliffe and Southover, not least 'John, Prior of the Priory of St Pancras Lewes and the convent of that place and all their men and servants'.

The Dissolution of the Monasteries closed the Priory and the Friary, bringing to an end their contribution to Lewes in education, hospitality and religious influence. Mary I attempted to bring England back to Rome, by violent means where peaceful ones failed. On 12 June 1555 an act of the Privy Council ordered the Sheriff of Sussex to implement the execution of three condemned people for heresy, 'being ordered to suffre in thre severall places of the shire; viz, one at Lewes named Derike, a berebrewer, and thother two at Steyninges and Chichester'. This Derick Carver, a Flemish brewer in Brighton, was the first of 17 men and women who were burned for their faith. None of the heretics lived in Lewes but the burnings gave an impetus to Protestantism locally. Their memory survives in Lewes's famous Bonfire Night celebrations, reaching back a half century before Guy Fawkes, as Cliffe Bonfire Society members carry 17 crosses in the procession and the Martyrs Memorial on Cliffe Hill is illuminated.

20   *West Gate, Lewes,* printed by G. Hullmandel with an imaginative High Street background.

21   Whipping Post and Stocks: Lewes Castle, postcard in the Grano series. These are no longer on display in the shell keep, but the fine 18th-century entrance to the west tower can be seen.

A curious tailpiece to the martyrs' story came in 1886 when Brighton Town Council were offered for sale 'the original gridiron that Richard Woodman and nine other martyrs were burnt upon on the 22nd day of June, 1557', which lay in the cellars of the *Star Hotel*, Lewes, from where it was sold about 1880 for £7-8. The local antiquarian, Mark Antony Lower, had seen it and thought it looked more like 'a rack for the stowage of good liquor'. In case the people of Lewes felt that they were missing out on their heritage, the Mayor of Lewes, Joseph Farncombe, wrote to the paper to cast scorn on the provenance of this artefact and concluded: 'Lewes Castle contains one of the largest and most interesting collections of antiquarian relics to be found in the South of England, and this gridiron would most certainly have found a place therein had there been good reason to believe in its genuineness.' Despite this, the gridiron was displayed until fairly recently in the kitchens of the Royal Pavilion at Brighton.

When England waited for the Armada, Lewes was the county's administrative headquarters, holding the arsenal which was six pieces of cast-iron ordnance, six carriages and nine pairs of wheels for the ordnance, 42 barrels of gunpowder and 120 cast-iron shot. With Lord Howard of Effingham, who was in charge of the English fleet, Lord Buckhurst was the joint Lord Lieutenant for Sussex and Surrey. In July he came to live in Lewes, at the Vyne which he had recently bought. He tried to muster the shire but only three of the rapes had responded when the Armada fleet sailed past the Sussex coast on the way to their rendezvous in the Netherlands. Then the winds blew, the enemy ships were dispersed and at Lewes the celebrations involved 'shooting of the great pieces in the castle', using two of the barrels of gunpowder. In 1590 there were rumours of another invasion, so Lewes was supplied with more powder and match, but this too was never put to the test, as the 16th century had no further storms to weather.

Two

Later Lewes Landmarks

John Rowe was the steward of the Manors of Lord Abergavenny from 1597 to 1622 and his accounts have survived to give an excellent picture of the life and local government of his time. Earlier records mention a merchant guild in 1140 and a provostory, but it is not until 1542 that the Society of Twelve, assisted by a Council of Twenty-Four, makes its appearance in written records. Rowe called them 'a society of the wealthier and discreter sort of townsmen' which had existed time out of mind, though their numbers were not as fixed as their names suggests. In 1542 their payments ranged from 8d. to the bailiff for discharging two sessions or buying arms and artillery to 6d. for giving two rabbits to the Duke of Norfolk's officers.

22 The burning of 10 Martyrs at Lewes, woodcut.

23 The Bonfire procession on High Street.

24 The Elizabethan coat of arms in the church of St Thomas à Becket, Cliffe, modelled in plaster in 1598 and repainted by E. Gordon Godfrey in 1932/3.

25 The Blunt cup, given to the town in 1611 by Thomas Blunt, though the earliest record refers to a bowl.

One of the Society of Twelve was Thomas Blunt, a barber-surgeon who died in 1611, leaving to the Constables and the Society of Twelve a silver bowl, double gilt, of the value of 20 nobles, as 'a pledge of his love to the townsmen of Lewes charity'. On 26 August 1611 Blunt also 'by his will gave his messuage in Lewes upon trust, and directed his trustees to pay out of the rents thereof £3 yearly to the free school of Lewes, and £3 yearly to the poor', i.e. £1 to the poor of St John under the Castle 'and the other ffourty shillinges yearely to the ffyve other parishes viz: St Michaell, St Mary Westout, All Saints,

26 The South Prospect of Lewes from *An Actual Survey of the County of Sussex* by Richard Budgen, 1721.

27   Keere Street, Lewes. Postcard by Judges' Ltd., of Hastings, showing the sign of Pinyoun the baker and grocer.

Southover and St Thomas in the Cliffe'. The endowment is now based on 171-172 High Street.

On 1 July 1642 Parliament directed that 20 barrels of powder for the service and defence of Sussex should be sold to Col. Morley of Glynde, the MP for Lewes. As the Civil War gathered pace, Captain Ambrose Trayton was given the power to call in 200 men, 'or more if occasion shall be, into the town of Lewes, volunteers or others, and to command the same for the defence of the said town'. Then

> the receivers of the propositions, money and plate, raised in the town of Lewes, shall detain in their hands a fifth part of the said monies and plate to be employed for the defence of the said town.

Four iron guns were recalled to Lewes that had been sent to Newhaven and Brighton in 1597, so that the town could protect itself. One report in late November 1642 said that in Lewes the townsmen and 300-400 men from the county rose for Parliament, 'but they want a head and leaders, and not one gentleman of that county offereth himself to do them service of that kind'.

The Parliamentarian cause had some opposition in Lewes: John Tufton, Earl of Thanet had acquired Lord's Place, on the former Priory site, and considered using it as a Royalist base, but dropped this scheme when he was defeated at Haywards Heath in 1642 with other supporters of the king. Thanet fled abroad and in 1654 had to pay £9,000 for the return of his lands, the largest amount demanded that year.

Ogilby's *Britannia* in 1675 reported that Lewes 'was esteemed the best borough town of the country' and 'chiefly composed of gentlemen's seats joining one another with the gardens adjoining'. Lewes from then on was at its peak as a market and county town, the period shown in the fascinating Lewes Town Model at Barbican House. Mathematical tiles began to adorn many of the buildings from about 1784, where they were used in the Friends Meeting House. They came in red, black and yellow, with an occasional grey, providing a lighter and cheaper alternative to brick. Brighton began to eclipse its proud neighbour, though ironically its prosperity owed much to the Lewes doctor, Richard Russell, who promoted the curative powers of sea water. The Prince Regent came over to Lewes from his Pavilion, to attend the Races or visit Col. Newton

28 Bull House, 92 High Street, home of Tom Paine from 1768 to 1774. Once known as 'the house with a monkey on it' from its distinctive corbel, a second was found in 1905 and reinstated.

at the Grange, and his desire to drive down Keere Street is well known.

Lower writing in 1870 of Bull House said that it was noteworthy 'as the residence for some time of Tom Paine, the atheistical writer of the *Age of Reason'*, who was then a local exciseman. He wrote that 'execrable book in this house, and the table on which he wrote it was, about fifty years since, in the possession of the late William Lee of this town.' Tom Paine came to Lewes on a salary of £50 a year in 1768 and found lodgings at Bull House. His landlord was Samuel Ollive who had a daughter, Elizabeth, who became Paine's second wife at St Michael's on 26 March 1771. Their marriage was terminated by a deed of separation on 4 June 1774, though Thomas 'Clio' Rickman maintained that Paine continued to send her money without letting her know who sent it. During his time in Lewes, Paine went to meetings of the Society of Twelve and to meetings of the Vestry which met across the road at St Michael's Church and elsewhere in the town. He also joined the Headstrong Club, still in existence, which met at the *White Hart* and was a weekly debating society of public-spirited Lewes citizens such as Rickman and William Lee who founded the *Sussex Weekly Advertiser,* or *Lewes Journal.*

29 Portrait of Tom Paine by Julian Bell in the Market Tower, 1999.

30 Mr. Thomas Clio Rickman, The Citizen of the World, a member of the Quaker family in Cliffe.

Paine was also a member of the Lewes Bowling Green Society. Played on part of the old bailey of the Castle, this club was founded on 4 May 1753 by Charles Boore 'for the better management of the old Castle Green on which the game of bowls has been played since time immemorial' and reformed on 15 April 1852 by the Subscribers to the Lewes Bowling Green. As the turf was not flat, the bowls have a heavier bias than modern woods. One author suggested that Paine got the idea of writing the *Rights of Man* from overhearing a comment at the Bowling Green by Mr. Verrall on the King of Prussia being all right as a king as he had so much of the devil in him.

Paine's time with the excise ended on 8 April 1774 and he left Lewes for greater things in

America where his radical writings on independence made him famous. He retained an interest in Lewes and wrote to the sheriff before a meeting at the Town Hall on 4 July 1792 on the suppression of certain books. He said that he had carried out his excise duties with,

> exceeding candour, and even tenderness ... The name of *Thomas Paine* is not to be found in the records of the *Lewes* Justices in any one act of contention with, or severity of any kind whatsoever toward the persons he surveyed, either in the Town, or in the Country.

He went on to say that he had 'many friends in Lewes, rich and poor, and most probably some enemies' but since leaving the town he had been

31 Lewes Castle from the Bowling Green, watercolour by Captain M.E. Musson, 1989.

32 The *White Hart* and *Unicorn Inn*, *c*.1865.

33 Lewes Bowling Green Pavilion and Players, *c*.1920s, photographed by E.J. Bedford. The names listed on the back are from left to right: Earp, Justice, Marsh, Downs, Morris, Dudeney, Jackson, Saunders, G. Holman, J.H.E. (?Every), Cecil Morris, Dr. Stokes, Philcox, Jackson, Jackson, (unknown).

34 Albion Street, looking north, photographed by Edward Reeves.

35 Fitzroy House, 1999.

thrown into a line of action that gave him wider insights, progressing to the implications of his *Rights of Man* and freedom. He died in 1809 but his memory is still very much alive, to be commemorated in his temporary home of Lewes by an exhibition in the town in 2000.

Free thinking was encouraged by reading and in 1785 the Lewes Library Society was established. For years it operated from a house in 3 Albion Street, with about 10,000 volumes, before moving to Fitzroy House in 1862, designed by Sir Gilbert

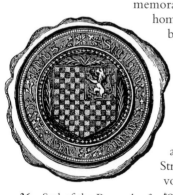

36 Seal of the Borough of Lewes, *c*.1835.

Scott. In 1897 the Shareholders of the Lewes Library Society contacted the Town Clerk 'suggesting that as they did not propose to carry on the Library after the present year the Corporation would perhaps take over the Fitzroy Memorial Building as a Public Library'. This was agreed and

> Alderman Kemp, J.P., very generously agreed to pay off the liabilities of the Library Society and the expenses, together with the cost of putting the building in repair, the total sum required for these purposes being probably from £200 to £300. On these favourable terms the Town Council have adopted the Public Libraries Acts.

The Fitzroy Memorial Library closed in December 1955 and the public library opened in the present building in Albion Street on 4 January 1956.

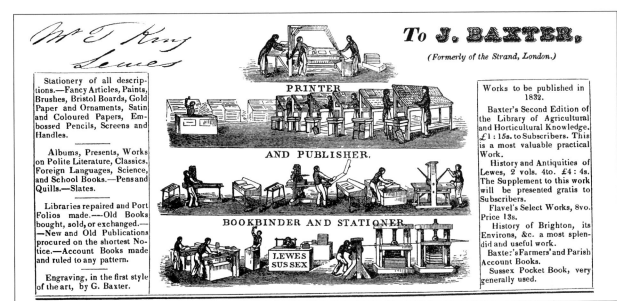

37   Invoice of J. Baxter of Lewes, 1831.

In 1806 the Town Act established improvement commissioners to pave, light, cleanse, watch, and repair the roads and other public places in Lewes, whilst protecting the rights of the lords of the borough. Lower commented in 1846: 'The qualification of a commissioner is the possession or tenancy of a messuage of £20 yearly value, or a personal estate of £800. The present number of persons who have qualified is about 112.' These men were able to levy a higher rate in order to do more extensive work, and in their first year the rates were 2s. in the pound. Cliffe followed suit in 1828 and Southover had inspectors of lighting in 1847.

In 1881 Lewes and its two satellites were formally incorporated into a borough, though not without resistance from some people in Cliffe. The new borough council had a mayor, six aldermen and 18 councillors, with Wynne Baxter as the first mayor of the Town Council. He had been the last Senior Constable of the old borough and was part of the famous printing firm in Lewes. He had been to the Home Office on 20 June 1881 to collect the charter of incorporation which he read at Lewes on 22 June. After this a procession headed by the Town Crier perambulated the new borough and the day inevitably finished with a grand torchlight procession and firework display.

This charter of 1881 defined the borough bounds as:

From the north-western corner of the wall of the garden of 'Malling House,' in a straight line to the point at which the old Turnpike Road from the Spital Barn to Offham crosses the road leading from the Inn called the 'Elephant and Castle,' in the Town of Lewes, to the 'Windmill', near the Race Stand, known as 'Steer's Mill,' or the 'Offham Mill;' thence southward in a straight line to the Windmill, known as the Spital Mill; thence in a straight line to the Smock Windmill, which is the most southerly of the two windmills, called the 'Kingston Mills;' thence in a straight line to the point at which the boundary of the parish of Southover crosses the Cockshot Stream; thence along the Cockshot Stream to the point at which the same joins the River Ouse; thence along the River Ouse to the point at which the same would be cut by a straight line to be drawn from the point last described to the point on the eastern Cliff known as the 'site of an old windmill;' thence in a straight line to the centre of the road, immediately on the north of the windmill called 'Malling Mill;' thence westward in a straight line to the aforesaid north-western corner of the wall of the garden of Malling House.

38 The Town Hall area celebrating the Diamond Jubilee in 1897; photo by Reeves. The *West Sussex Gazette* wrote that to celebrate the event in Lewes, 'The Fitzroy Library was taken over (by the liberality of Alderman C.R. Kemp) and the Libraries Act adopted: a recreation ground was formed on the Town Brook and will be taken over by the Corporation; the erection of a nurses' home, an increase of funds of Victoria Hospital and a bust of Queen Victoria for the Town Hall are also in hand'. The Borough's costings for this programme were £180 for the Recreation Ground, £320 for the Nurses' Home, £450 for the Victoria Hospital and £100 for the bust. That was delivered to the Town Hall, but the health spending was delayed.

39 *Star Hotel* and Bank House before the *Star* was transformed into the Town Hall.

40 North side of the High Street, looking west, *c*.1880.

The new Town Hall was built by Denman of Brighton and opened in 1893,

> at a cost of about £17,000, is of red brick and Portland stone, in the Renaissance style: the old oak staircase, adorned with various carved figures, is one of the chief features of the building: the upper floor comprises the council chamber, mayor's parlour and various offices; new offices were added in 1914. The assembly room measures 83 by 48 feet, and is 32 feet in height, with an organ chamber at the north end, and will seat about 200 persons. The Corn Exchange, on the east side of the building, is also available for entertainments &c. and will seat a large number of persons.

The tours of the building give a fascinating insight into the civic life of the town.

In 1894 the town was divided into three wards with six councillors each and reallocated in 1934 as Bridge Ward, Castle Ward and Priory Ward. The next change saw the establishment of Lewes District Council which now covers 113 square miles from Saltdean and Seaford up to Newick and Wivelsfield and is 'a multi service organisation committed to providing high quality services to those who live and work in the area'.

Lewes has long been the county town of Sussex. In describing the County Hall of his time in 1835, Horsfield wrote: 'The old Town Hall, which stood near the centre of the High Street,

41   Assembly Room, Lewes Town Hall.

42   Old Town Hall, Lewes, 1761, drawn by W. Scott and printed by Baxter.

43   Diamond Jubilee celebrations, 1897, photographed by Bartlett, showing the High Street from the old County Hall on the left to the Town Hall topped by a flag.

was pulled down by virtue of an Act of Parliament, passed in 1808, and the present Shire Hall or Sessions House erected.' At that time county business mainly involved the administration of justice at the Quarter Sessions and Assize. When the County Council came into being in 1888, more rooms were added at the back. As the Council expanded, so did the need for space and various plans were floated, from acquiring Newcastle House next door, which was agreed, to a

new building on Castle land, which was not. The final solution of building a new County Hall at the top of the town has not met with universal acclaim. In 1926 East Sussex County Council also took over Pelham House and added the Council Chamber, Committee Rooms and offices in 1938.

No bureaucracy can prevent natural disasters, such as the avalanche of 27 December 1836. Charles Wille, who lived nearby, recorded in his

44 'The Lewes Avalanche', an oil painting by Thomas Henwood, representing the scene of the avalanche at the time of the second fall, with men running away with the injured and the lookers-on in the foreground.

45   The *Snowdrop Inn*

This Tablet

Is hereby given by Subscription to record an awful instance of the poor uncertainty of human life, on the morning of the 27th of December, 1836, by the poor-houses of this Parish. Was destroyed by a Mass of Snow falling from the hill above, and the following Eight individuals were Buried beneath the ruins :---

William Geer, 82.   M. A. Brighman, 28.

Phœbe Barnden, 45.   Jane Boaks, 25.

Mary Taylor, 42.   Joseph Wood, 15.

Susan Hayward, 34.   Mary Brighman, 11.

Their remains are interred on the North side of the Church.

" Be ye therefore ready, also for the Son of Man cometh at any hour when ye think not."

46   Tablet in South Malling Church to the victims of the avalanche.

---

diary for Boxing Day that a great fall of drifted snow had fallen into his timber yard, 'driving the upper Saw house nearly to the front of the Yard, breaking down the upper end of the Shed'. He tried to persuade those living nearby to leave their homes, but few responded. The next day, he wrote: 'Between 10 and 11 in the Morning a great fall of Snow took place opposite Bolder Row (the parish houses), forced them down, and burrying in the Ruins fourteen persons, 8 of whom were taken out dead.' Neighbours immediately rallied round to help the survivors. The tragedy is perpetuated in the name of the *Snowdrop Inn*, built near the site on South Street in 1840. The two-year-old Fanny Boaks survived and the dress that she was wearing at the time is now on display at Anne of Cleves House, near Thomas Henwood's painting of the scene.

Lewes had gas from 10 September 1822, provided by the Lewes Gas-Light Company whose manufactory was

for preparing and producing inflammable air or gas, from coal and other materials, and of applying the same to the lighting of the town of Lewes, and parishes of Cliffe, Southmalling and Southover ... and of preparing and obtaining Coke, Coal-Tar, Pitch, Asphaltum, Ammoniacal Liquor, Essential and other Oils, and other Products of such Coal, or other materials.

The works were on the river bank in the Cliffe and the company was incorporated in 1845.

47 Cable laying outside the Town Hall, 1900, photographed by Reeves.

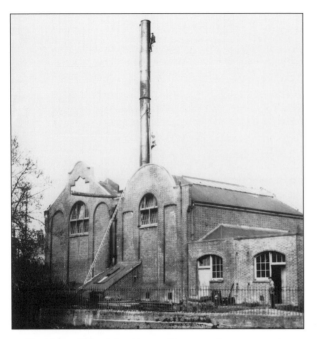

48 Lewes Electricity Power House under construction at Bear Yard, photographed by Bartlett.

The next utility was electricity and in 1890 the local paper recorded one of many meetings of the townspeople to consider street lighting. The Mayor had been on fact-finding missions to other towns and 'could not hold out any hopes of having electricity cheaper than gas'. Charles Wells reminded the meeting that he had exhibited the electric light in 1878 and 1879, as well as pointing out that Brighton produced its gas much more cheaply than Lewes. The meeting came to no firm conclusion, except to ask the Gas Company to reduce its prices, and it was 27 September 1899 before the Highways Committee agreed to the Electrical Power Distribution Company Limited's offer, which was finalised in 1900. Street lighting was the responsibility of the Town Council who commented in 1906 that the number of lamps had gone up to 255 as opposed to 187 in 1882.

The town expanded in the 20th century. The Avenue was constructed about 1907, originally as D'Albiac Avenue, but altered at the request of the residents in 1908. It had been parkland, known as the Wallands and owned by the Shelleys of

49 Lewes soldiers at Lewes Station, 1918; photograph by Bartlett of men standing in front of an LBSCR carriage.

Lewes, and took its original name from George D'Albiac who married a Shelley in 1806. When Miss Cordelia Shelley, the last of her family to live at the house now known as Shelley's, died in 1854, her property passed to her D'Albiac nephews. The parkland beyond Shelley's Paddock, which formed part of the estate, became the subject of building speculation, with roads named after contestants at the Battle of Lewes, and was completed as the Wallands. Building in and around De Montfort Road was rather piecemeal: St Mary's Terrace in 1864, Summervale Terrace in 1888 and Shelley Terrace in 1906.

In the First World War, Lewes men signed up with the same loyal enthusiasm as elsewhere. George Holman, the first freeman of the Borough of Lewes, published *Some Reminiscences* in 1930 and recalled from his house, The Rowans:

> When the late Earl of Chichester went on active service he nominated me to take his place on the County Territorial Force Association, on which I served until his return. Lewes had a vivid reminder of war power conditions when over 12,000 men were dumped into the town in less than 48 hours. Trains were constantly arriving, day and night, packed with men from the mining and other districts, some of them taken straight from the pits in working garb, to be billeted in every part of the town. The normal population was suddenly doubled and every house had to share the responsibility of the sudden invasion.
>
> As chairman of the County Hall Committee I had to arrange for billeting in that building. The council chamber, committee rooms, courts of law, corridors, and even the forecourts were packed with men, numbering over a thousand. (To relieve the congestion I took 25 men to my house for several weeks, where I boarded and lodged them.) The Town Hall, parish rooms, old workhouse, Corn Exchange and every available shelter was occupied; and for a few days the men had to lie on straw, until army blankets, etc. arrived.

No photos were allowed, so this remains an unusual record. Holman also remembered that 'train loads of munitions were running day and night through Lewes to the harbour for shipment, and no attempt was made by enemy craft to blow up the enormous stores of shells deposited there.'

After the Armistice, the Borough of Lewes decided to commission a monument at the top of School Hill to record the names of those who had died in the First World War. The site had been occupied by St Nicholas Church which was removed in 1792 and its bell, Gabriel, became the town bell, now in the Market Tower. Mrs. Dudeney's Diary for 22 January 1919 stated: 'There has been a town meeting over some memorial to Lewes soldiers who have fallen. One illuminated idiot suggested an obelisk with a urinal and cloakrooms underneath.' Happily, this was not approved and an open competition was arranged with an honorarium of £50 for the winner who in a field of 35 was Vernon March of Goddendene in Kent, whose family were well known for cast monuments. His maquette which won him the competition was found accidentally under a bench in the March brothers' studio in 1977 and was on display at Anne of Cleves House. The full-size bronze monument by the March brothers was unveiled in an impressive ceremony on 6 September 1922 and the cost of £2,000 was raised by public subscription. The service today as the forerunner of the Bonfire Night celebrations every 5 November is a moving moment in a hectic evening.

Mrs. Dudeney's diary for September 1939 gives a feeling of what the coming of another World War meant to the average resident. She had problems with blackout as her house was so high that it could be seen all over Lewes, but by 7 September 'not a bit of black stuff to be had and 21 windows to be darkened'. 6,500 evacuees came to Lewes and Mrs. Dudeney sat on Brack Mount that September, watching

> what seemed an endless procession of children all with gas masks and with their small belongings, sometimes in pillow cases or sacks, on their little backs. All being shepherded by voluntary helpers with white armlets. In the case of RC children by nuns. These children were shot in at the particular houses which had been allotted to them, but the householders nearest on the route had the pick. And I was told that one poor boy—big for his age and about fourteen—was left until the last. I suppose they thought he would eat too much.

One of the evacuees, Bryan Hart, was evacuated from Croydon to Lewes on 4 September by train and 'marched to All Saints Hall at the bottom

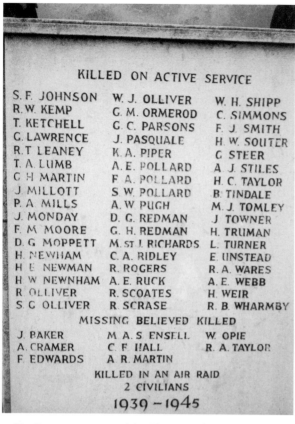

KILLED ON ACTIVE SERVICE

S. F. JOHNSON	W. J. OLLIVER	W. H. SHIPP
R. W. KEMP	G. M. ORMEROD	C. SIMMONS
T. KETCHELL	G. C. PARSONS	F. J. SMITH
G. LAWRENCE	J. PASQUALE	H. W. SOUTER
R. T. LEANEY	K. A. PIPER	G. STEER
T. A. LUMB	A. E. POLLARD	A. J. STILES
G. H. MARTIN	F. A. POLLARD	H. C. TAYLOR
J. MILLOTT	S. W. POLLARD	B. TINDALE
P. A. MILLS	A. W. PUGH	M. J. TOMLEY
J. MONDAY	D. G. REDMAN	J. TOWNER
F. M. MOORE	G. H. REDMAN	H. TRUMAN
D. G. MOPPETT	M. ST J. RICHARDS	L. TURNER
H. NEWHAM	C. A. RIDLEY	E. UNSTEAD
H. E. NEWMAN	R. ROGERS	R. A. WARES
H. W. NEWNHAM	A. E. RUCK	A. E. WEBB
R. OLLIVER	R. SCOATES	H. WEIR
S. G. OLLIVER	R. SCRASE	R. B. WHARMBY

MISSING BELIEVED KILLED

J. BAKER	M. A. S. ENSELL	W. OPIE
A. CRAMER	C. F. HALL	R. A. TAYLOR
F. EDWARDS	A. R. MARTIN	

KILLED IN AN AIR RAID
2 CIVILIANS
1939–1945

50 Lewes war memorial with names from the Second World War, 1999.

of Station Street. There we were given something to eat and drink and arrangements were made to find foster homes in and around the town.' He had two homes before arriving in Landport and recorded:

> At the start of the war, building work on the initial plan for a council estate on a site known as Landport was still in progress. The estate site stretched from Arundel Green, at one end and some fields, adjacent to a farm, at the other. The farm was on the edge of some woods, through which a twisting country path led to Offham Church. The land between Arundel Green, Offham Road and Wallands Crescent was occupied by allotments.

On 5 October 1940 Mrs. Dudeney noted:

> The Nazis have at last found Lewes. 9 [10] bombs this morning. One in Southover demolished Mrs. Jones's memorial to her husband; one behind Martin's garage blew up a car; one, a time bomb, in a house on Chapel Hill, so all the dwellers on Chapel Hill are, for the time being, evacuated.

The next day she observed that soldiers too were billeted in Lewes House, so that Walter Godfrey, who had been living there, retired to the stable block, 'Thebes'. After a lull she was

51 Second World War troops marching past County Council Offices at Southover House.

able to record *The Big Raid on Lewes* on 20 January 1943 and two days later she saw the

> most awful devastation in the town, especially in North Street, New Street and New Road. The *Stag Hotel* burnt to the ground and Stevensons the Corn Chandler has lost his windows with almost the last lovely fanlights left in Lewes. All the people have got to clear out of St Martin's Lane, which also was hit.

Many people have been proud of Lewes, but until recently not everyone was prepared to take practical steps to save it. Mrs. Dudeney wrote in her diary for 2 June 1944:

> Caroline Byng-Lucas came looking very decorative as usual. ... They are having a meeting at Miller's on the 28th with the view of forming some sort of society for preserving old houses in Lewes, should they be threatened. She told me—and I hadn't seen it—that after Lewes was bombed last January twelve month there was a notice put up in the window of the Southdown bus office. 'Do not fret. You will have a larger and a lovelier Lewes, after the war.' God help us! She also told me that Mr. Godfrey had said that he, they—the Byng-Stampers and Mrs. Dudeney—were the only people who cared a hoot about preserving old Lewes.

Nothing is permanent and one shop front from Lewes High Street was presented by C.N. Pickup to Hull in 1936, to take its place in a museum of shops. Conversely, one of the highlights of 1999 was the return of the great cultural icon, *The Kiss* by Auguste Rodin. It was commissioned by Edward Perry Warren, a rich American aesthete who bought Lewes House in 1890 and supported many local institutions. He was a keen swimmer and helped to improve the Lewes Corporation Swimming Baths where he took his regular early morning dip.

Rodin's marble masterpiece was brought to Warren's attention by William Rothenstein who saw the first version in 1900 and offered a contract of £1,000 for another. Rodin came to Lewes in 1903 to see Warren's collection of Greek antiquities. On 28 November 1904 the 4½-ton marble left Paris on its way to Lewes, where it was housed in the coach-house for the next ten years, apart from one trip to be exhibited in London. In 1914 Warren offered to lend *The Kiss* to Lewes Town Council, making the journey

52 'Old Shop Front from Lewes, Sussex, Now in Course of Re-erection in Hull', from a measured drawing by Walter Godfrey, 1936, of the shop front of Messrs. Lowdell, Cooper & Co., ironmongers who bought the premises in 1812 from Messrs. Molineux & Steward. Ironically, it was destroyed in a wartime bombing raid on Hull.

BY ORDER OF H. ASA THOMAS, Esqre.

LEWES HOUSE,
LEWES, SUSSEX.

In the Centre of the Town, within 5 minutes from the Station
(main London-Eastbourne line).

SALE OF THE VERY VALUABLE

Contents of the Residence

(*as collected by the late* E. P. WARREN, M.A.),

comprising Rare Examples of

15th, 16th, 17th and 18th Century Furniture

Old English, Continental & Oriental China & Porcelain.

Over 900 ozs. of very fine Old Silver & Sheffield Plate,

BEAUTIFUL OLD EMBROIDERIES, BROCADES AND RUGS.

Rare Old Music.   A remarkable Old Fireback.

A FEW CHOICE EXAMPLES OF EARLY PAINTINGS.

Antique Bronzes, Grecian Columns and Ivories.

Rodin's Famous Marble Group "Le Baiser"

AND MANY OTHER INTERESTING WORKS OF ART.

TO BE SOLD BY AUCTION, ON THE PREMISES, BY

ROWLAND GORRINGE

On Tuesday, Oct. 22nd, 1929, and two following days.

Sale to commence on the First Two days at TWELVE o'clock
and at ELEVEN o'clock on THURSDAY.

Private View, by Card only, Thursday, October 17th (10–4).
On View, by Catalogue only, Friday, Saturday and Monday, October 18th, 19th
and 21st (10–4, each day).

Catalogues (1/-, illustrated 2/6) from the AUCTIONEER, 154, High Street, Lewes, Sussex.
'Phone 505.

Farncombe & Co. (1923) Ltd., Printers. Lewes.

53 Sale Catalogue for Lewes House, October 1929.

54 'The Kiss' in the coach house of Lewes House, alongside other treasures accumulated by Edward Perry Warren.

from Lewes House to the Town Hall on a trolley, pulled by three men and four horses. It was installed in the Assembly Room on 2 December 1914, a space which was then given over to troops billeted in the town. Boxing matches were held there and *The Kiss* provided an excellent vantage point on which to stand for a better view. It was then covered up, to avoid offending local sensibilities and returned to the stable block at Lewes House where it stayed for 16 years. Warren died in 1928, leaving Lewes House and its contents to his secretary, Harry Asa Thomas, who auctioned them through Rowland Gorringe on 22-24

October 1929, but incredibly *The Kiss* failed to reach its asking price. Eventually it was offered to any provincial gallery prepared to pay for transport and insurance, and Cheltenham Art Gallery accepted it on loan. In 1939 it was loaned to the Tate Gallery who purchased it in 1955 by public subscription. The Tate generously allowed *The Kiss* to return to Lewes from June to October 1999, to be exhibited at the Town Hall alongside comparable works by Rodin, where it was seen by some 73,000 people, a fine high point on which to bring the 20th century full circle.

Three

Lewes and its Rivers

The water routes of Lewes have been used for centuries. The presence of Quarr stone from the Isle of Wight as an early building material suggests water-borne transport. This method of transport was used when the Normans imported stone from their homeland: in 1227 the bailiffs at Seaford were directed to allow one vessel to go free, when the Prior of Lewes was sending to Caen for stone to build his church. Later, when a French ship landed at Seaford during one of the many wars between England and France, it was captured by the locals who released it on hearing that its cargo of Caen stone was bound for the Priory. At that time, boats could deliver the stone quite close to the Priory, meaning that only a short distance needed ferrying by cart. Chalk was mined from Cliffe for the Archbishop of Canterbury whose customers included the Prior of Lewes, who paid him ten shillings for chalk in 1530. From the quarry in the cliffs at Southerham came chalk to make mortar in Edward IV's reign, and in both cases river transport would have helped. The port at the mouth of the Ouse changed in the mid 16th century as Newhaven took over from Seaford, but the river route to Lewes remained busy.

The structure described by John Rowe as 'the Bridge commonly called Lewes Bridge over the Great River' was a vital trading link for those on either side of the Ouse. The original crossing may have been a ford, but there is a mention of bridge repair in 1159. The earliest bridges were made of wood, which would often need repair. The money to maintain them came from the Rapes of Lewes and Pevensey, and much later Hastings Rape became involved. In 1563 John Chatfield was the surveyor of the works for the new bridge, which had begun in 1561, and he received £87 5s. 3d., besides 50 shillings for 'preferring a bill into the Parliament House, for the preservation of great timber'. In 1564 the Lewes Constables recorded a further payment of 41 shillings for work on the bridge and in 1584 'Lewas Brige this yeare was New Bylded'. A meeting of the general quarter sessions in Lewes on 18 July 1650 heard that this bridge needed repair and the estimate was £80, towards which the Borough of Lewes was rated at £11 3s. 10d., a sum which was authorised to be collected by 10 June 1651. In 1712, Eastbourne's Parish Book recorded a payment of £1 8s. 0d. to rebuild Lewes Bridge.

When one night in the great floods of January 1726 the wooden bridge was washed away, it was decided to build something more substantial. A replacement in stone and brick was built by the local mason and Lewes Constable, Arthur Morris, whose son John followed him in both careers. The designs were by Nicholas Dubois who was the architect of Stanmer House, where Morris had worked for four years. The bridge opened in 1727 and was paid for by charges on Lewes and Pevensey Rapes. Not everyone paid these dues happily, Hurstpierpoint for instance

55 Lewes Bridge, 1781.

56   Race at Cliffe Bridge, photographed by Bartlett after the bridge improvements of 1908.

objecting to the request for £30. Paul Dunvan approved of the bridge as he saw it in 1795, calling the architecture 'remarkably neat and strong, and is objectionable only for its narrowness'. He felt that it was likely to stand without any considerable repairs for some centuries to come, and he was right.

The narrowness of the ten-foot carriage road was widened by adding footways and the bridge was modified to take account of the widening of Cliffe High Street following the passing of a new law in May 1828. This had been undertaken to counteract the threat from the Trustees of the Malling Roads who wanted to build a bridge over the Ouse at the end of North Street, which would have seriously affected Cliffe's monopoly. Their enterprising reaction to the external threat meant that they retained their monopoly on the river crossing, which remained unbroken until 1969 with the construction of the Phoenix Causeway and the new road bridge.

Further work on the bridge in 1908 and more fundamentally in 1932 give us the form that can be seen today.

Lewes as a port had been busy for centuries, coping with the products of local agriculture as well as industries. In 1382, for instance, Walter atte More was appointed to the office of controller of the customs of wools, hides and wool-fells, the threepence in the pound, and other petty customs due from merchants in the ports of Lewes and Chichester. As trade developed, many were able to take advantage of river transport to become successful. Between 1613 and 1638 Ralph Akehurst, a Cliffe merchant, traded coastwise in groceries and grain and overseas with Ireland, Dieppe, Calais and Flushing in grain and other commodities, finding time to be churchwarden at St Thomas's and bully his wife Mary. John Stansfield, the maternal grandfather of John Evelyn, had a long career between 1580 and 1613 when he exported iron and grain to the west

57 Monument to John Stansfield and his wife Jane in All Saints; drawing by Grimm.

[2547]

ANNO TRICESIMO PRIMO

Georgii III. Regis.

CAP. LXXVI.

An Act for improving the Navigation of the River *Ouse*, between *Newhaven Bridge* and *Lewes Bridge*, in the County of *Suſſex*; and for the better draining of the Low Lands, lying in *Lewes* and *Laughton Levels*, in the ſaid County.

 WHEREAS the River Ouſe is at preſent navigable from Newhaven Bridge to Lewes Bridge, in the County of Suſſex, foɀ ſmall Barges, and at certain Times of the Tide; and by widening, deepening, and rendering moɀe ſtraight, the Current of the ſaid River, by new Cuts oɀ otherwiſe, the ſame may be made navigable moɀe conſtantly, and foɀ Veſſels of a larger Burthen, whereby the Trade and Commerce upon the ſaid River will be conſiderably increaſed, and the Publick

Preamble.

5   28 R 2

58 An Act for improving the Navigation of the River Ouse, 1791.

country and wheat to Marseilles, and imported salt, wine and fish.

Where there was wealth, so were there thieves and a letter of assistance survives from the Privy Council on 4 October 1579

> of a process granted out of her Majesty's principal Court of the Admiralty for the recovery of certain goods taken by Samuel Bigges, alias Hollande, and his company from John Harman and others of the town of Lewes in Sussex and for the apprehension of the pirate himself and his companions.

The watermen held their traditions dear. On 24 August 1767, the *Lewes Journal* recorded:

> At the Assizes on Tuesday last, came on a cause, where in Mr. William Marten on behalf of the Lady of the Manor of Newhaven was plaintiff, and a servant of Messrs. J & R Burtenshaw of this town Defendant,

concerning an ancient customary right claimed by the Barge-owners, & navigators upon Lewes river, to take Beach Gravel, Sand, &c at Newhaven for the use of the Town of Lewes and other places bordering upon the river without paying anything for the same, when after a trial of five hours & hearing many learned arguments on both sides, the Jury found a verdict for the Defendant whereby the custom is established.

It was not always plain sailing and the weather often made conditions difficult or worse. In January 1776 a snowfall made the roads impassable and the Ouse froze over, which was great for the skaters but less good for people with a living to earn. On 28 January, the local paper recorded: 'The Bargemen carried a boat in full sail through the Town to raise money, being out of employ, the navigation of the river Ouse being obstructed by the Frost. They got a

59 Lewes Floods, Lewes Station, London Line, November 1960, photographed by W.K. Rector.

60 Lewes Floods, Lewes Station, Platforms 1, 2 & 3, November 1960, photographed by W.K. Rector.

liberal contribution from the inhabitants.' Samuel Durrant of Southover gave beef and soup twice a week during the hard weather to 'all who chose to accept it'.

As the 18th century progressed, it was felt that better water navigation was needed in the clay country about Lewes 'so as to bring corn to market in winter from a dirty country surrounded with turnpike gates' and for carrying chalk and other manures for land improvement. The Company of Proprietors of the River Ouse Navigation became official in 1790, with the aim of making the Ouse navigable from Lewes Bridge up to Lindfield, at their own expense, though they were authorised to impose tolls. With a renewed interest in leisure, this stretch of the river is again being considered for development. Heading seaward, on 6 June 1791 Parliament passed 'An Act for improving the Navigation of the River Ouse, between Newhaven Bridge and Lewes Bridge, in the County of Sussex; and for the better draining of the Low Lands, lying in Lewes and Laughton Levels, in the said County.' This announced that the river was navigable to Lewes Bridge 'for small Barges, and at certain Times of the Tide: and by widening, deepening, and rendering more straight, the Current of the said River, by new Cuts or otherwise, the same may be made navigable more constantly'. It also improved 'other Streams running into the River Ouse, and by the Works herein before mentioned as requisite to be erected for the Improvement of the Navigation of the said River, the Drainage of the low Lands in the said Levels will be materially affected'.

This proved to have both commercial and sanitary benefits. Horsfield commented in the 1830s:

> In speaking of the improvements that have recently taken place in the town and its vicinity, it is impossible not to dwell for a moment on the almost incredible good that has been experienced by the inhabitants at large from the judicious and well executed improvements in the navigation of the river, the funds for which are contributed in equal proportions by the commercial and agricultural interests of the town and land adjoining, under the management of Trustees. Instead of the Levels being now as formerly overflowed four months in the year by the union of land and sea floods, a few hours are generally sufficient to draw off the inundating

waters. If even the soil had not benefited by the change, the inhabitants of the villages skirting the estuary certainly have. Agues which within the memory of every adult were the curse of the villagers, have decreased in proportion as the efficacy of the drainage has increased: whilst in the town itself, but especially in the Cliffe, where this distressing disease was formerly very prevalent, it is now more frequent than other diseases, depending on marshy miasma. The advantages which the commerce of the town derives from the improved navigation of the river can be duly estimated by every tradesman. Much praise is certainly due to Mr. Ellman for his well devised and ably-executed plans.

Despite the improvements, flooding still happened. In December 1801 there was a building in Swing-pump alley, later North Court, which contained unslaked lime: when the river flooded it, there was very nearly a disastrous fire but the blaze was brought under control. Thomas Woollgar noted that the highest flood in Lewes in his memory was on 29 January 1814

> after a thaw of snow. When the water came into Cliffe Church & stood above a foot deep in the Belfry. In consequence there was no service in the Church the following day. The water was at this time so high at the Wheat Sheaf in Malling Street that a Cart plied to carry passengers to and fro the road.

The most dramatic floods came in November 1960. Because of excessive rain in October, when 8 inches fell instead of the average of 2.78 inches, the water level was too high to allow the swollen Winterbourne stream to empty itself into the Ouse as normal. It therefore overflowed in Southover, flooding the cattle market and the streets and houses in the vicinity. By 4 November the water had invaded the railway station to the extent that the electricity for the live third rail had to be turned off and the Hastings and Brighton lines were able to operate only by using steam engines. This was photographed by W.K. Rector who also wrote up the events for *Sussex Notes and Queries*, where he said that 620 homes were thought to have been flooded, plus business premises, with the total damages amounting to about £300,000, worth a great deal more then than now. The Ouse rose three feet above street level in Cliffe and Malling, so families had to be evacuated and businesses suspended until

61   Fête Day at the Pells, photographed by Bartlett.

the water level dropped. Amphibious vehicles were called in to take people to safety and the Mayor set up a disaster fund. Even Bonfire Night had to be abandoned and it was two weeks before the water level dropped sufficiently before the Brighton Road, cut off at Falmer, could be re-opened.

The Pells represents a different use of water in Lewes. It may originally have been a swannery for the monks of Lewes Priory and much later it was the site of a paper mill used by the Lewes printer Arthur Lee and his partner Thomas Johnston, who opened the mill in 1802 by the Hogbrook below the church of St John sub Castro. This did not last and in 1860 came the Swimming Baths, constructed by public subscription, making it a very early example of an open air public baths. It has survived, despite many attacks, and is much loved by many Lewesians. The land on which the Pells stands was given to the town by John Rowe when he was Constable of Lewes in 1603 and his much later successors, Robert Crosskey and Henry Card, added to this in 1879. Sawyer in 1897 described the Pells as

> a beautiful piece of ornamental water, fringed with trees, quite a fine collection of water-fowls will be found here, including swans, Chinese and Sebastopol geese, pochards etc. etc. Water Lillies flourish here also. A water carnival, or illuminated procession of boats, took place in the Pells recently, and although the water is very shallow, the fête was a grand success.

62 Ship building at Lewes, with a boat under construction, middle right.

Alderman Wynne Baxter, the town's first mayor, handed over the Pells to the town in 1920 'in recognition of the kindness he had at all times received from the inhabitants of his native town'.

Lewes had a small but thriving ship building industry for a brief period in the 19th century. In March 1839 the first sea-going vessel was built there: the 61-ton brig *Lewes Castle* was launched from the yard of Rickman and Godlee. Hundreds turned out for the naming ceremony, which was performed by Mrs. Johnson, wife of one of the four owners—Johnson, Farnes, Monk and Lidbetter. Wille's diary described the launch on 10 January 1840 of Mr. Berry's barge, 'named the *Penny Post*—this being the day when Postage was reduced to a Penny'. On 27 July 1843 he noted the launch of Mr. Berry's vessel, the *Mary Ann*, though he noted on 28 February 1848 a day which was 'very wet and blowing. Mary

Ann wreck'd off Rotterdam, lading with wheat'. Among other ships built at Lewes was the topsail schooner, *Wallands*, launched from Chatfield's Bridge wharf on New Year's Day 1866, which carried what was probably the last cargo of tree nails from Lewes to the Baltic.

Barges travelled the river with cargoes of coal, corn, loam, cement or iron and steel destined for Every's Wharf and the Phoenix Ironworks. These works were founded in 1832 at the bottom of North Street but moved to the site near the bridge before moving back to North Street. Generations of John Everys owned the works, the most memorable in the town becoming mayor and a collector of Sussex ironwork which he left to the Sussex Archaeological Society. He also left to the town a Playing Field of five acres on the old Paddock, with its Pavilion dedicated to the memory of Mrs. J.H. Every.

63 Barges unloading near the Phoenix Iron Works.

64 Advertisement for Phoenix Iron Works, 1875.

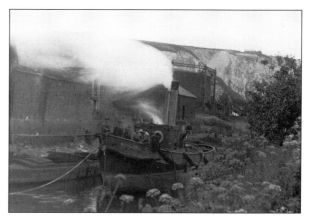

65 The Newhaven Steam Fire Launch *Haulier* in action at the fire which destroyed the *Bear*, 18 June 1918.

66 The aftermath of the fire of 18 June 1918, damaging the footbridge from the warehouse of Charles Aspull Wells, ironmonger.

Other works in the town benefited from the river, not least the cement works which moved to Southerham in 1929, having started in 1902 near the *Snowdrop Inn* as the Lewes Portland Cement Company.

Two tugs in the early 20th century helped to bring sea-going vessels and river barges into Lewes and, as traffic eased off in the 1920s, Newhaven fishermen sometimes helped to tow the sea-going barges upstream. The boats that could use the river needed to negotiate the bridges, with water levels and seamanship being critical factors. This did not always work, as the S B *Shamrock* was involved in a jamming incident under Cliffe Bridge in March 1937. Prior to that, on 18 June 1918, the Newhaven Steam Fire Launch *Haulier* came to help to fight the fire at the *Bear Hotel* and Strickland's granary but ran aground opposite the Gas Works on her way upstream, stopping 200 yards short of the fire, though she remained to damp down the fire until the late afternoon. The beginning of the end came in the 1930s when the railway was electrified, so that the bridge at Southerham could no longer be raised and coal barges changed to unloading at Piddinghoe.

Water was needed not only as an avenue for commerce but also for drinking. At first the formalisation of this was a little haphazard: in 1829 the Visiting Magistrates of the House of Correction thought about using

> some of the Female Prisoners and the supernumerary Male Prisoners in working the Pump at the House of Correction whereby the Water for the Town might be

conveyed from thence up the Town as high as the Market Place if a Tank or Cistern were permitted to be placed there for the Commissioners of the Town to take the Water therefrom into the Watering Cart.

The plan failed as no-one erected a water tank.

Many places had their own wells and the inventory of Lewes Castle in 1397 mentioned 'a bucket with rope for the well'. Others such as Cliffe relied on a local supply. Horsfield wrote that, at a vestry meeting of 24 July 1804, it was resolved, 'that a parish pump should be erected near the church porch, by subscription, and that the remainder of the money wanted for the purpose, should be paid out of the poor rates'. The meeting on 3 October 1804, resolved, 'that on account of the great public utility of the said pump, particularly to the poor, and in case of fire, the whole of the expense should be paid out of the poor rates'. The pump was erected close to the church porch but, when the market house was pulled down, it was moved to the east end of the church. 'It is supplied from a well in the centre of the high road, leading up the hill, at about twenty yards from the Cliffe corner. The water is of very excellent quality, and conduces much to the comfort and health of the inhabitants.'

Horsfield later gave notice that

> a Company is about to be formed to supply the Town with Water, from a Tank, to be placed near St Ann's Church, which will convey water to the top rooms of the houses. It will be supplied from the Cockshut Spring, a water of the purest quality.

Lower recorded the next stage:

> By an act passed 3 & 4 William IV, a company was empowered to construct reservoirs and lay down pipes to supply the town with water. The water, which is of the purest quality, is derived from a copious spring in the parish of Kingston, and immediately contiguous to Southover, whence it is forced by a low pressure steam-engine to a reservoir about 90 feet high, on the opposite eminence, for the supply of the lower parts of the Town: and to another near St Anne's Church, 150 feet high, for the accommodation of the higher parts.

When the Lewes Waterworks Company started to sink a tank about 100 yards west of St Anne's

67   Southerham Bridge, Lewes starting to open to allow a boat from Every's Iron Works to be towed to Newhaven, 1906.

68   Southerham Bridge, Lewes; a boat just passing through bridge.

69 The Pinwell drinking fountain after it was moved across the road in 1874.

the Parish of All Saints' had it cleared out, an arch turned over it to cover it and a Wall built to protect it at his sole Expence—In the year 1839 the Well being nearly filled up with rubbish John Hoper Esquire of the same parish had it again cleared, completed the wall and had it furnished with a Door and strong lock and an Iron Pump properly fixed at his sole expence to the great convenience of the neighbourhood. ... Mr. Hoper directed that the key of the door to the Well should be placed in the hands of the Senior Churchwarden in trust for the parish.

In 1874 'this pump was moved to the opposite side of the Road, and a Drinking Fountain was erected by subscription the Land belonging to the Constables on which it stood together with a Spring Well was enclosed planted and Walled in.'

Animals, too, needed water. The *Lewes and East Sussex Church Magazine* for August 1869 commented favourably on the experimental troughs at Malling and Cliffe which 'were a great boon to the cattle during the time they were in use from July to December 1868. Sometimes 200 drank at them in one day and therefore the Committee feel most reluctant to give up the proposal'. Metropolitan troughs appeared elsewhere in the town later and were much appreciated.

People were beginning to realise the importance of clean water in the fight against disease, though it usually took an epidemic to raise public awareness. *The Town Book of Lewes* for 16 August 1866 recorded a public meeting at the County Hall in Lewes to consider 'the propriety of collecting Subscriptions towards a Fund for the relief of Districts affected by Cholera', which resulted in the establishment of a Committee to look into the problem. In 1874, Wille noted that the usual 5 November celebrations took place on 30 December, 'being put off on account of the sickness at that time. The latter part of the year the Town was visited with a serious illness, suppos'd to arise from the water work—many dying in consequence.' The results of a survey in 1897 were published and the sample of water from the Waterworks, at Verrall's pool, was declared 'perfectly free from sediment and suspended matter. I consider it to be a water of high-class purity and one that may be safely used for drinking and all other domestic purposes'. Wartime

church for the waterworks in 1834, it hit a pre-Christian burial-place with both skeletons and cremation urns, plus a variety of animal bones.

The source of water at Pinwell was thought to be a perennial spring and gave its name to Pinewell Street in the late 13th century.

This Ancient Well being in a ruinous state in the year 1812, Mr. William Attwood of

70   The Pumping Station; photograph by Bartlett of building which was demolished to make way for the pavilion of the Stanley Turner Recreation Ground off the Kingston Road.

71 Boats arriving at Bridge Wharf by Harvey's Brewery, photographed from Lewes Bridge by Bartlett.

72 Harvey's Brewery yard under water, 1909, photographed by Bartlett.

emergencies called for drastic measures and in the Second World War, when the Bowling Green was requisitioned, a static water tank was installed in the south-east corner.

During his visit to Lewes in 1822 Cobbett reported a comment of John Ellman who said that when he 'began business, forty-five years ago, every man in the parish brewed his own beer, and that now, not one man did it, unless he gave him the malt!' Pubs sometimes had their own brewing facilities, a trend that has re-emerged thanks to CAMRA, but it could be risky: Wille reported on 9 July 1844: 'A Lad fell into Bear Brewery Copper while boiling and died in the course of the day'.

Messrs Lyell Bros ran the South Malling Brewery and visitors in 1893 were assured that 'the firm's operations were carried on under perfect hygienic conditions. There is an abundant supply of good, pure water, and only the best of malt and hops are used, the whole being under the supervision of one of the firm.' Breweries could be both seen and heard: at a meeting on 3 June 1896 the proceedings of the Finance and General Purposes Committee were approved,

> except the Resolution recommending the Council to sanction the use of a steam whistle by the Southdown and East Grinstead Breweries Ltd. Put and lost … Further amendment … except that the Southdown and East Grinstead Breweries Ltd be allowed to sound a whistle six times a day instead of 10 times a day … Put and lost. Original carried Corporate Seal to be fixed to the two sanctions to use steam whistles.

On the riverside stands the only brewery to survive, having started in 1790. Its founder, John Harvey, worked at Thomas Wood's Brewery in Lewes and also began to acquire inns. On Wood's death in 1838, Harvey bought the Bridge Wharf for £3,707. The reporter in 1893 commented on Messrs. Harvey and Son's brewery, 'which is one of the finest buildings, and most extensive business premises in the town of Lewes. The office is in High Street, Cliffe, and the brewery premises lie at the back of it, close to the banks of the river'. This was certainly true, and many photos survive to show the river closer to the brewery buildings than was intended. The brewery buildings were altered in 1881 by the London architect William

73 Demolition of chimney at Verrall's Southover Brewery, 16 September 1905; postcard by Bliss of Lewes.

BEARD & CO. (LEWES) LTD

BREWERS AND BOTTLERS   -   IMPORTERS OF WINES AND SPIRITS

TELEPHONE - 193

For about 150 years, Beard's popular ales have been brewed at the Star Lane Brewery in Fisher Street. The illustration shows the back of the Brewery on both sides of Castle Ditch, a view well-known to numbers of Lewes people who habitually use it as a short cut to the High Street. It is a curious fact that the premises are situated in three parishes.

74 Advertisement for Beard & Co.'s Brewery from *Lewes: The Official Guide to the Historic County Town* by Walter Godfrey, *c*.1938.

Bradford. In 1893 one observer wrote:

> The establishment may be taken as affording a good type of the best class of country breweries, well up to the public demand. ... The premises are conveniently situated for business, close to the river, and within easy distance of the railway. The firm are also coal merchants on an extensive scale, supplying their indispensable commodity in any quantity.

Harvey's remain in Lewes, creating special ales for the modern taste, sometimes with names from the past such as Tom Paine, and their popular brewery tours give an idea of why they have succeeded so well.

Messrs Frank Verrall and Sons ran the Southover Brewery which had been in the family for centuries. When it was sold in 1916, Mrs. Dudeney wrote in her diary about 'old Verrall who meant to sell his brewery business for not less than £70,000. Sold it for £120,000'. This same site figures in Mrs. Dudeney's diaries in the Second World War as well, when the Rector of Southover on 4 July 1944

> told Mrs. Jervis that the Old Brewery House, occupied in the war by a German called Schwartz (who ran a button factory at Barcombe Mills) has lately been altered in some way and behind one of the walls they found a transmitter. So the Button Factory was only a blind. He was a spy.

Messrs. Beard & Co. ran the Star Brewery on Fisher Street which in 1893 was described as flourishing in a quiet sort of way as they had for the previous hundred years, formerly as Beard & Chitty. In recent times the Star Brewery has an entirely different function, acting as a base and display area for many artists and craftsmen in the region, catering for a different kind of recreation.

Four

Lewes and its Roads

In 1970 the Friends of Lewes submitted to the Lewes Joint Steering Committee its concerns about traffic in the town centre. Their first concern was damage to the buildings:

> The great increase in through traffic has brought a new menace to the town's buildings. In the view of the Society failure to remove through traffic from the town within the next five years would result in irreversible damage—traffic not only hastens physical decay to building structures but prevents the arrest of decay by making repair and improvement economically unattractive.

Few would argue that these worries were unfounded then or now, especially when observing the regular struggles of buses or lorries manoeuvring along the High Street, past parked cars and angry pedestrians. Lewes suffers the same fate as many old towns, built to accommodate very different traffic. This did not include

75 Traditional means of transport into 18th-century Lewes; engraving published by A. Morris of Lewes.

juggernauts or petrol fumes or holes being dug in the road for one service or another (but rarely both at the same time).

Nathaniel Paine Blaker, writing of the Lewes he knew in 1843, said:

76 Malling Street, Lewes in the early 19th century; drawing.

45

77 The fireback of Richard Lenard, showing the tools of his ironworking trade, on display at Anne of Cleves House. Other examples of this design are known, but none so complete.

In the days before railways, Lewes was the main artery through which nearly all the traffic between east and west Sussex passed, as well as that to and fro Brighton. There was no other bridge over the Ouse either up or down the stream for some miles, and the High Street of Lewes was therefore a very busy place. Besides the ordinary traffic, which was of a very considerable amount, coaches, four-in-hand, 'Unicorn' and pair-horse, both from east and west, were constantly dashing through the town; the pace at which they went down School Hill and the rattle they made can scarcely be imagined: and to this must be added the crowds at the booking-offices and sometimes the scramble for places.

To reach the area now filled by the town of Lewes, travellers for thousands of years had used the South Downs ridgeway. This route was lined by many Bronze-Age round barrows, which were visible against the skyline, and the Romans used this as the basis for their route east from Chichester. Since 1963 parts of this ancient trackway have become the South Downs Way, running from Eastbourne towards

Winchester and the Pilgrims Way. The name of Juggs Lane at the end of Southover High Street commemorates the old route which brought the fisherwomen from Brighton along Kingston Ridge passing the *Juggs Arms* in Kingston towards the old West Gate of Lewes, their donkeys loaded with panniers or juggs, full of fish.

The ancient forests of the Weald to the north with their heavy clays were much more difficult to cross, though the Romans created roads to service the iron industry and give access to the coast, particularly for their wheat which was exported to the Continent. One of their roads headed south from London through Ashdown Forest to Cliffe and another through Hassocks and Clayton. Their road making was so efficient that the routes survived for centuries, helping the growing Sussex iron industry and requiring a specific width for cart wheels in the hope of minimising damage to the road surface. In 1266 the murage grant made to Lewes allowed the inhabitants to raise money through tolls to repair the battle damage: every horseload of iron for sale from the Weald nearby paid a halfpenny in toll and every cart laden with iron paid double. A similar murage grant in 1334 perpetuated this, along with charges on other goods such as corn and cloth.

Gradually man imposed his order on the landscape so that travel could become less of a struggle, though emergencies still occurred. Lord Buckhurst, as joint Lieutenant of Surrey and Sussex, was faced on 18 April 1600 with the need to transport the governor of Dieppe from Newhaven to London, with an entourage of 100 people. They stopped overnight in Lewes while Buckhurst tried to meet their travel needs. He wrote to Sir Walter Covert, the nearest deputy lieutenant, asking him to assemble as many of the gentlemen as he could, then go to the governor to meet his needs.

> And I have sent one other letter to Grinsted Town in Sussex which is 14 miles from Lewis and is the next Town in which he might either renew his horses or lodge all night—written to the constables there (for there is no justice near by 7 miles) to se him and his trains furnished with horses and all things he shall desier fit for him.

The rest of the journey was left to the devices of the other Lieutenant, Lord Howard of Effingham.

It was recognised that streets in the town needed to be kept clean. In 1595 a bye law penalised every householder in Lewes High Street who did not keep the street clean 'before his door after due warning from the Constables, Headboroughs or scavenger' when a fine of 6d. was enforced. In 1607 another bye law laid down that 'the owner of any hog permitted to wander in the streets or lanes of the town, shall forfeit 6d. for every such offence against the safety and cleanliness of the town' and the following year there was a further law against 'laying dung or any other noisome matter within forty feet of any dwelling house, or within ten of any stable or barn, under penalty of 10d.'.

In those far off days before the Internet and mobile phones, communication depended on human endeavour. A message about shipping in the Channel in 1630 was transmitted from Lewes to London by a messenger on foot, but horse-drawn transport was also possible. By the 1750s the Post Office advertised a service from London to Lewes, via the somewhat circuitous route of Arundel and Brighton. In the 1750s this operated four days a week, but in the next decade it was daily. Edward Tasker was responsible for receiving and dispatching posts in Lewes. He combined this with being a peruke maker, so people called at his barber's shop to leave their letters, often crossed to save paper but not the recipient's eyesight. Tasker's son Thomas was paid just over £40 a quarter for this Post Office work, which he sold in 1778 to Samuel Dunstone who also ran a shoe warehouse and carried on the business at 56 High Street into the next century, despite an abortive attempt in 1791 to set up a regular mail coach service.

Defoe's observations give some idea of the reality of 18th-century travel:

> Here I had a sight, which indeed I never saw in any other part of England: Namely, that going to church at a country village, not far from Lewis, I saw an ancient lady, and a lady of very good quality, I assure you, drawn to church in her coach with six oxen; nor was it done in frolic or humour, but meer necessity, the way being so stiff and deep, that no horses could go in it.

The heavy oxen will have added to the problem of the road surface, as did the timber which was pulled from Sussex to the Medway and the journey could take three years if the summers were

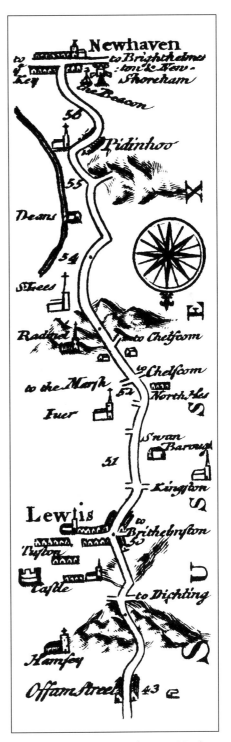

78 The Road from London to Newhaven; Emanuel Bowen's adaptation in 1751 of John Ogilby's road map of 1675.

wet! Lewes was a victim of its own success as a commercial centre, as shown in the case of John Fuller, the gunfounder of Waldron, who wrote in 1743: 'I have gotten twenty 9 pounders of 9 feet to Lewes. These have torn the roads so that nothing can follow them.'

There were other hazards, too, as shown by a newspaper account in October 1751:

A few days ago, as the Rev. Mr. Hincliffe was passing over the South Downs, on his way to Lewes, he was attacked by two ruffians on foot, who pulled him off his horse, and took out of his pockets a Common Prayer Book, a guinea, some silver, and a ring off his finger, his hat and wig; and then pulled a cord out of their pockets, and tied him by the neck to a stump, and then left him.

He was found over eight hours later by Tom Cordwell, a poor shepherd, who released him, found him a horse and asked for his prayers.

Mr Hincliffe told him that he would not only remember them in his prayers, but as

soon as he got to Lewes, he would send them a proper gratuity for their kindness and hospitality, as he did not know but it was (under God) owing him that his life was preserved.

From the Highways Act of 1555, parishes had been responsible for the upkeep of roads within their boundaries, overseen by the local justices at quarter sessions. Sussex had one advantage in road construction as the road makers were able to make use of the plentiful slag heaps from the Sussex iron industry. The 17th-century practice was revived in the 18th century when tollgates replaced the old bars or pikes across the road, and Sussex had its first turnpike road in 1749. The Turnpike Act of 1752 sought to remedy the quality of the roads north of Lewes, announcing that 'the roads are in so bad a condition that they are impassable to wheeled carriages in winter and very dangerous and difficult for persons travelling on horse-back'. The House of Commons passed a Bill for repairing the road from 'the North end of Malling Street to Wych

79 View of Lewes; an 18th-century etching of the road into the town.

Cross, and to Broil Park Gate. And from Offham otherwise Wogham to Wych Cross'.

In 1770 there was a petition to the House of Commons from Sussex travellers,

> setting forth, That a Road leading from the Town of Lewes, to the Town of Brighthelmstone, in the said County, is in some places very bad, and in other Parts very narrow and incommodious, and cannot be effectually repaired and widened by the Laws in being: And therefore praying, That Leave may be given to bring in a Bill for repairing and widening the said Road, in such Manner as to the House shall seem fit.

Giving evidence to substantiate this, Mr Josias Smith described the road from Lewes to Brighthelmstone as 'in some parts very bad, rough and stony, and in other parts very narrow and incommodious'. The House agreed that the road should be repaired. In 1770 the Lewes-Brighton Turnpike Trust was set up and ran the road from 'Irelands Lane, Lewes, to opposite the Bear Public House where the parishes of Brighton and Preston join' and it continued until disturnpiked in 1871.

Stage coaches plied their trade between Lewes and London and competition gradually built up. In 1756 James Batchelor's New Machine operated on the London-Brighton route, calling en route at the *Star* in Lewes. In 1762, Tubb and

**LEWES & LONDON
Original Stage Waggons,
BY SHELLEY,**

Load at the GEORGE INN, Borough, every WEDNESDAY, and at the WHITE HART, INN, Borough every SATURDAY.

Forward Goods to the undermentioned Places:

LEWES,	BLATCHINGTON,	FIRLE,	STANMER,
NEWHAVEN,	ALFRISTON,	GLYNDE,	OFFHAM,
SEAFORD,	WILMINGTON,	RINGMER,	CHAILEY,

AND ALL PLACES ADJACENT.

The above Waggons set out from LEWES, every MONDAY and, THURSDAY Morning.

The Proprietor will not be accountable for any Money, Plate, Watches, Writings, Jewels, Glass, or China, however small the value may be, unless an Insurance be paid above the common rate of Carriage. Nor more than Five Pounds will be paid for any one Package of other Goods, not specified above, except entered & paid for accordingly. Will not be accountable for any accident that may happen to Carriages drawn at the end of the Waggons; nor any live Animal, though lost, hurt, or killed.

80 Advertisement in the *Lewes Journal* for Shelley's Stage Waggons.

Browne advertised their 'Lewes & Brighthelmston new flying machine on steel springs' which made the journey from Charing Cross on Mondays, Wednesdays and Fridays, stopping at the *White Hart* in Lewes. This took two hours less than Batchelor who responded with a New Flying Chariot with cheaper prices for the journey. Joseph Farington travelled from London to Brighton on 23 October 1793, via Croydon, Godstone, East Grinstead, Uckfield and Lewes. In his diary he recorded: 'It is a longer distance than either of the other two roads, by 6 or 7 miles & the stage from East Grinstead a very

81 Marking the miles to London, stone plaque built into the wall of the 15th-century Bookshop, High Street, but formerly across the road.

heavy road. We were 10 Hours and ½ going.' A new London to Brighton route opened via Reigate which did not touch Lewes, but there was still plenty of business and two coaches left Lewes for London every morning, with waggons doing the journey every Tuesday and Friday. Occasionally people attempted to take short cuts with the law and in November 1795, Nicholas Linn, a carrier from Brighton, was convicted of 'letting Two Horses for hire to be used in Travelling Post by the Day', from Brighton to Lewes and back, 'without having a Post Horse Licence so to do'.

In July 1770 one traveller, Sally Bradford, recorded the costs of a return journey between London and Sussex to collect her young daughter. The journey by coach to Lewes from the Golden Cross at Charing Cross in London cost her 6s. 6d., plus the hire of a horse and man to continue the journey from Lewes to Eastbourne, which cost 7s. 0d. On the return journey from Lewes to London, the journey cost 9s. 9d., travelling outside the Lewes Machine coach service. The Lewes Machine left the Golden Cross at 5 a.m., stopped to allow the passengers to have breakfast at the *White Hart*, Godstone, before continuing to Lewes which was reached at 3.30 p.m., where the travellers could have dinner at the *White Hart*.

People living in the villages around Lewes had to make their own arrangements. Thomas Turner, the village shopkeeper in East Hoathly, had to make regular seven-mile trips to Lewes for his business, on parish matters and socially. He would either walk, which took about three hours, or hire a horse from someone in the village and pay the turnpike 2d. This could be hazardous. On 10 December 1755, 'about 3 o'clock went down to Mr. French's and borrowed his little horse to go to Lewes upon for wine for Dame Reeve's funeral, having sent for some but it did not come as I expected. I rode him up home to put on my greatcoat etc., and accordingly got up at the block, but by accident, either by touching him with the spur or his taking fright of the dog, he fell a-kicking and running etc. and threw me down near the corner of Mr. Virgoe's stone wall, and hurt my side very much'. Return traffic operated similarly: on 8 August 1755 he 'paid the post 2d. for bringing a parcel for me from Lewes'.

In 1846 Lower told his readers:

There is a coach to London, leaving Lewes at 10 on Monday, Wednesday, and Friday, and arriving at 5 on the alternate days. The *Brighton* coaches are numerous, thus maintaining an hourly communication between the 'Queen of Watering-places.' Offices, Leney's, High Street, and Ticehurst's, High Street. A coach from Brighton to *Tunbridge Wells*, through Lewes, three times a week. A coach daily from Brighton to *Hastings*, Sundays excepted. A coach from Brighton to *East Bourne* three times a week. Further particulars it would be useless to give, as the arrangements are continually varying.

By this time the threat was not from another coach service but from the railway.

When the Rev. Edward Boys Ellman looked back to the Lewes of his youth, he recalled that

the whole of the streets were paved with boulders. I think it was about 1823 that the boulders were taken up and the roads macadamized. The boulders, however, remained in some of the side streets for many years, and I am not sure whether some of the steep lanes leading from High Street on the south side are not still so paved.

Other roads needed to be changed, too. Malling Hill replaced a route that had become very dangerous for travellers coming in from the Eastbourne direction, along a steep slope past the Lynchets, or another via Spences Lane and Church Lane. Horsfield recorded of the Malling and Ringmer roads:

To complete the general improvement of this neighbourhood, the Road Trustees, abandoning their former design of a new bridge, undertook in 1830, to make a new turnpike, so as to pass over Malling Hill at a point of which the elevation is less by about 55 feet, and the situation about one furlong westward of the old summit. The steepness of the ascent on both sides is by this alteration reduced to less than one half. In fact, on the north side, it is quite inconsiderable.

One of the characters of Malling Hill was Miss Mary Hannah Rickman, the horse-loving member of the important Quaker family who lived at Spence's, the house later known as The Grey House. Her relative E.V. Lucas wrote of her:

82 Malling Hill, with the Prince of Wales in the foreground and Malling Mill in the background; postcard by Brooker of Eastbourne and postmarked 11 July 1910.

This lady had such a humane feeling for horses, that she would make an irresistible offer to any driver who seemed to her unsympathetic; and then provide the overworked animal with pasturage and comfort for life, and after its death give it the honours of burial. The story went that astute costermongers and gypsies, wishing to make a little extra money, would flog their beasts near her gates, in spite of the notice set up there:

Uphill, whip me not;
Downhill, hurry me not,

hoping that the humane Miss Rickman would emerge purse in hand: which she usually did.

Miss Rickman's regard for horses may have been extreme but such care was needed. Five days after the avalanche of 1836,

> a fly belonging to Mr. Stevens went out of Lewes on Monday with a fare; but when the empty vehicle reached Ringmer Gate, on its return, the snow was over the palings; the driver, therefore, got home as best he could on foot. Mr. Stevens went with assistance to extricate his horse, but finding it could not be done, he mercifully spared the poor animal the misery of dying from cold by shooting him outside.

When not required on active service, horses could be put to pasture or housed at Cox's Livery Stables behind the High Street, where in 1893 some 40 hunters waited patiently in new mews for their London owners to come down and take

83 Working horses at Pannett's on Westgate Street, with the entrance to Pipe Passage in the bottom left corner.

them to a meet in the area. Cars on the other hand were viewed by many as a mixed blessing. On 9 June 1914 the vigorous rector of St Michael, the Rev. Henry Belcher, wrote to the local paper to demand a speed limit and describing an incident he had witnessed by the Freemasons' Hall on the High Street:

> in one of the most frequented and dangerous Narrows of Lewes, a motor cycle of two passenger capacity flashed by at the rate ... of 30 miles an hour. ... People were moving about, children and women especially, bound for their several places of worship. ... The fellows passed like a streak. The ordinary user of the streets here appears to be as helpless against these outrages on common neighbourliness and decency as we are all against Militants.

No doubt he would have approved of the speed bumps installed as part of the recent traffic calming measures.

The arrival of motorised transport brought with it not only the pressure on the roads and hard-won garage space, but the problem of parking. *The Official Guide to Lewes*, edited by Walter Godfrey in the early 1930s, recommended parking at The Cliffe, Morris Road, Albion Street, Abinger Place, Southover Road, Rotten Row and Friars Walk. Sixty years on, the problem is not resolved and can undermine moves to increase tourism within the town.

In 1927 the *Sussex County Magazine* published an interview with the Mayor of Lewes, Councillor Arthur Norman Innes, who was proud of the town of which he was first citizen, including

84 A more sedate ride past what is now the Bow Windows Bookshop on the High Street, which would not have worried the Rev. Henry Belcher.

the street improvements that had been occupying the attention of the Council. He told the interviewer: 'You will readily understand that the narrow streets of Lewes, and the buildings of 100 years ago, were not planned for the heavy motor traffic of today.' The article went on to explain that 'the congestion at Cliffe corner had become acute, but an abrupt corner on the spot where the traffic from London, Hastings and Eastbourne meets has been rounded off and the roadway widened, and the remaining site is available for the erection of high-class business premises'.

When the East Sussex Federation of Women's Institutes produced a book of memories, one member living between Falmer and Kingston recalled:

> The postman came out from Lewes on his bicycle to deliver to the local farms and houses, and PC Baker from the village would frequently pass by on his bicycle heading for Lewes to report to his superiors at the police

station there. He was even passing by one night in 1944 when a Mosquito fighter plane which had been shot down crashed on the roadside.

The newspapers arrived by Southdown bus and were thrown over the garden wall by the conductor, while the bus driver waited for him to do this service each day on their way to Brighton. ... You could go almost anywhere from Lewes on the buses which passed along the A27, Ringmer, Eastbourne, Tunbridge Wells and many more of the local villages.

In 1965 the town council installed a pedestrian bridge over the river near the Pells which cost £4,000 to ease the journey from the Malling Estate to Lewes town centre. Then, before the medieval road systems seized up completely from the density of modern traffic, an inner relief road and a by-pass were planned to relieve congestion, the latter forming part of

85   The inside of Martin's Motor Garage, Lewes. Martin's business began here in 1904 and the site is now Riverside.

the A27 which accommodated the coastal traffic. The bulk of the inner relief road was abandoned in 1970, but one element was built, by-passing Cliffe High Street and linking with a new river crossing, a 24 ft.-wide road bridge, whose design was approved by the Royal Fine Art Commission.

The *Evening Argus* of 4 April 1974 reported that the Department of the Environment had announced the route of the by-pass, essentially as published in December 1971 except that the crossing of A275 Kingston Road would not have a roundabout. There had been a great many objections but the line chosen ran 'from the A27 Brighton Road through Hope-in-the-Valley through a cutting to Winterbourne, across the plain of the River Ouse close to the south

side of Lewes, to a roundabout at Southerham on the A27 east of Lewes'.

There are two entrances to Lewes off this road. One brings traffic to the Prison cross-roads from the Kingston turning, where stood a pair of early 19th-century Round Houses at Ashcombe Gate in turnpike days. The other travels through the Cuilfail Tunnel, at an estimated cost of £1,648,000, and past the snail sculpture. There it meets the road from Uckfield and the east, cutting Malling Street in two and removing cottages, including three former ale-houses. At one point in 1979, the *Evening Argus* reported that the work on the 11,300 ft. long and 22 ft. wide tunnel seemed to be threatening 'expensive houses on the exclusive Cuilfail estate', but this was resolved. On 10 August,

ON the site of a Millwright's Works, where, possibly for centuries, Sussex Windmills were built and repaired, are now Showrooms and Workshops, equipped with the latest devices and machinery for servicing the modern Motor Car.

NEW CARS. SECOND-HAND CARS
REPAIRS AND ALL CAR SUPPLIES

85–97 WESTERN ROAD, LEWES

Phone 1221-1222   Telegrams : Lumotors

86   Advertisement for Lewes Motors Ltd. on Western Road, from *Lewes: The Official Guide to the Historic County Town* by Walter Godfrey, *c.*1938.

87 Shaw's shop at Cliffe Corner, at the junction of Cliffe High Street and Malling Street, mentioned by Cllr. Innes.

88 The toll house at Ashcombe just west of Lewes in 1826 by George Baxter.

89 The Cuilfail tunnel, opened on 11 August 1979.

90 The snail sculpture.

the day before the tunnel opened to traffic, it opened to pedestrians for one day and many people took the chance to investigate this new road tunnel on foot. The snail is really an ammonite and celebrates the engineering feat of mining the tunnel through the fossil-laden chalk which keeps the traffic away from South Street. One hundred and fifty years earlier, schoolboys had gone along to watch the engineers blasting through the chalk for the cutting for the railway line to Hastings. C. Underwood Jenner recorded that

we found fossils among the fragments and took hammers with us and broke them up. At one time I had quite a collection and, among others, ammonite shells, one of them as big as a large plate, and smaller shells, very like scallops, and quite a number of sharks' teeth as smooth as glass embedded in the stone.

The modern ammonite is a happy thought to relax motorists waiting in the traffic at this corner.

Five

Religious Life

The settlement evidence for Lewes before 900 is slight and there is even less for the religion practised. One possible clue is the pit burial illustrated in Horsfield's *History of Lewes* of the Roman urn with cockerel bones, bones and teeth from a boar, horse, mussel and oyster shells. This was dug in 1814 by Dr. Gideon Mantell from the back of his Castle Place garden when he was trying to prevent the castle walls falling into his property, but he could not follow this up for fear of bringing down the whole tower.

Pre-Christian burials survive in Lewes, sometimes on ground that was later consecrated for Christian use. St Anne's and St John sub Castro

both have clear evidence of this, associated with mounds that may have been part of early settlement. The *Sussex Agricultural Express* of 25 May 1839 described the workmen's impromptu excavation of the mound to the south of St John's:

> When they reached the centre of the crown of the Mount they exposed a circle of burnt earth, of two rods in diameter, around the sides of which were a few burnt human bones and a large quantity of boars and animal bones also burnt. On the east side an urn of baked clay was found, and also a spear head or iron weapon; showing that the Mount was an ancient British barrow, and

91   St John's Church, Sussex, 1785.

92   Bronze boar, found locally.

93   Carved stone of Magnus, St John sub Castro.

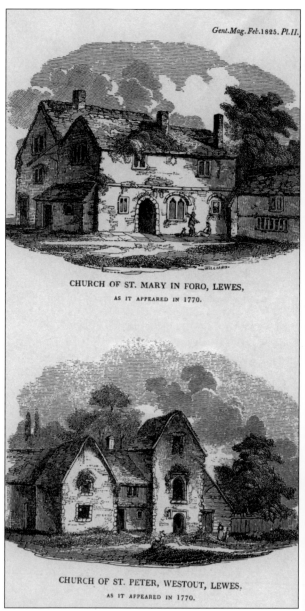

Gent.Mag. Feb.1825. Pl.II.

CHURCH OF ST. MARY IN FORO, LEWES,
AS IT APPEARED IN 1770.

CHURCH OF ST. PETER, WESTOUT, LEWES.
AS IT APPEARED IN 1770.

94   The churches of St Mary in Foro and St Peter Westout as they appeared in 1770, from the *Gentleman's Magazine*, February 1825.

that long before Christianity was introduced into England, St John's church yard was a scite for Druidical sepulchres.

The reference to boar bones in both excavations is fascinating, as small bronze boars appear to have been venerated in the Lewes area before the Romans arrived.

No Lewes church is mentioned in Domesday Book, though St John sub Castro may have existed then, not to mention the original wooden church of St Pancras, where the Priory was later built. The late Saxon monument to Magnus in the churchyard of St John sub Castro once stood by the chancel door, but that was pulled down in

H. C. WOOLMORE

Tobacconist & Cigar Merchant

49 HIGH STREET

*T*HIS was formerly the ancient Church of St. Mary-in-the-Market, at the top of the Old Market Place of Lewes, and next St. Mary's Lane (now Station Street). At the union of the parishes of St. Mary and St. John, in 1538, it became the Parsonage, and the building remains much as it was in that year of the reign of King Henry VIII . . .

THE MOST CONSPICUOUS SHOP IN LEWES

ITS REPUTATION MATCHES ITS POSITION

95 Advertisement for the building which had been St Mary's, from *Lewes: The Official Guide to the Historic County Town* by Walter Godfrey, *c.*1938.

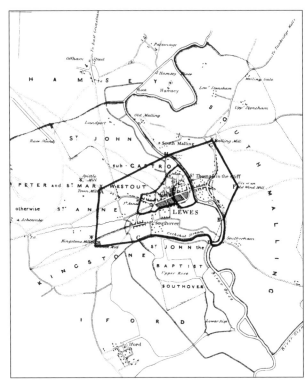

96 Map of the parishes of Lewes in the early 19th century.

1587. Magnus's monument was fixed in the outer wall in 1635, thanks to John Rowe who collected together the defaced pieces. Horsfield quoted the tradition that he was a Danish general who was converted to Christianity and became an anchorite. Others prefer him to be the son of Harold II and the antiquarian John Elliott quoted the suggestion that Harold was not killed in 1066 but escaped and came here.

A document of 1337 lists 14 churches in Lewes, perhaps to help the Bishop of Chichester to amalgamate some of the parishes, though this was not done. Four were outside the walls: St Peter Westout and St Mary Westout, which later both formed St Anne's Church; St John the Baptist

in Southover and St Thomas à Becket in Cliffe. This was originally a chapel of ease and under the patronage of the Archbishop of Canterbury, so was not answerable to Chichester as the rest were. Inside the walls St John sub Castro was probably the oldest, and the rest were St Peter the Less, Holy Trinity, St Nicholas in Foro, St Sepulchre, St Mary in Foro, St Andrew, St Martin and St Michael. Some survive in street names off the High Street.

Ten were in the patronage of the Prior and Convent of St Pancras, Lewes but none had a closer link with the Priory than the church of St John the Baptist at Southover. It began life as part of the guest house of the Priory but by 1263 it was a secular chapel which moved to its present location outside the Priory gates in the 14th century and became the parish church. It survived the destruction of the Priory, though the tower fell down in 1698 and was replaced in a different style. Inside in 1847 it acquired a neo-Norman chapel to house the remains of the Priory's founders, discovered during the making of the railway

97 'Southover Lewes' by R.H. Nibbs.

98 The Warenne cemetery, Southover Church, Lewes.

cutting, and the tombslab of Gundrada, retrieved from Isfield Church in 1775.

Lewes in the 13th century was part of the diocese of Chichester. In 1244, Henry III obtained the election to this vacant see of Robert Passelewe, archdeacon of Lewes, a worthless man who, according to Matthew Paris, 'had obtained the king's favour in a wonderful degree by an unjust inquisition by which he added some thousands of marks to the royal treasury'. The Archbishop of Canterbury refused to confirm the election, preferring Richard de Wych, so the case had to go to Pope Innocent IV who decided in favour of Richard and consecrated him on 5 March 1245.

The new bishop carried out his duties very forcibly. His confessor Roger Bocking recorded that he compelled

> a knight who had sacrilegiously imprisoned a priest, to swear to obey the commands of Holy Church. He forced him under oath to carry a set of wooden stocks, to which he had tied the priest's feet, on his shoulder like a beast of burden carrying its yoke, through the market-place at Lewes and around the church in which the priest who had suffered this outrage had served, and refused a great sum of money offered in commutation of this penance. He also compelled some citizens of Lewes, who had violently forced a thief out of a church where he had taken refuge and hanged him, to dig up the thief, or rather his decaying corpse for he was now dead and buried, and carry him to church on their shoulders.

The accomplices were beaten and he compelled them 'to go naked save for a shirt and breeches into the market-place of Lewes and other nearby towns with ropes around their necks', again refusing money instead of punishment.

St Richard was also an admirer of goodness in others and, when he died on 3 April 1253, he left in his will: 'To the female recluse of the Blessed Mary of Westoute at Lewes five shillings.'

During restoration work in 1927, her bones were disturbed and Mrs. Dudeney went with her friends on 1 November 'to the reburial of the bones of the anchoress at St Anne's. Simple affair: just a bishop in cope and mitre, a few prayers, then "May she rest in peace" and "May light perpetual shine upon her". Moved me profoundly' though the argument about the anchoress's Catholicism did not.

During a visit to Lewes, this saintly bishop went up to the Archbishop of Canterbury's bailiff who was standing on Lewes Bridge supervising a group of fishermen. The bailiff said to him: 'My lord, we have toiled a long time here and have caught nothing. If it please you, wait here a short while and, when we have brought in our nets, bless them so that we may let them down once more with your blessing'. The saint smiled, raised his right hand and blessed both the water and the fishermen and said: 'Now let down the net in the name of the Lord'. The fishermen did this and dragged the net through the water. When they hauled it back on land, they found four fine mullet, which are usually found at sea. The saintly bishop 'ordered that the fish which they brought to him should be given to the Friars Minor who lived in that town, for he claimed that it was on their account that God had given these fish'.

These friars were members of the new Franciscan order who came to England in 1224. The building work at the Lewes Friary was in progress in 1242, when the friars were granted timber from 10 oaks. Henry III gave them permission in 1243 to ask the burgesses of Lewes to allow them to build a wall over to the town ditch to enclose their precincts. Part of this precinct wall was still in place in the late 18th century when Gideon Mantell remembered it ablaze with wallflowers, red and white snapdragons and vipers' bugloss.

When the Dissolution was imminent, Cromwell was informed on 9 December 1537 that two Grey Friars had been saying that the King was dead. One, Friar Richard, confessed that he had heard the rumour from 'a somyner who keeps an alehouse opposite the Friars' Gate' and told Friar Longe and Black Herry. He was kept under guard and on 29 December Sir William Shelley was able to tell Cromwell that 'the friars have their punishment this Saturday at Lewes, and take it very penitently'. It was never a wealthy house and when it was dissolved in 1538, its assets were insufficient to cover its debts. When the site was excavated in the 1980s in advance of building the new magistrates' court, it disclosed eight periods of activity on the site, plus 55 medieval burials.

The Cluniac monks of Lewes Priory belonged to the richest monastery in Sussex with revenues of £1091 9s. 6d. Their final months at Lewes were dominated by both lay and religious matters.

99   The Friars Lewes, The Property of Mr Nehemiah Wimble by whom this plate is presented, 1825.

100   'St Pancras Priory Gateway, Southover' by Thomas Henwood, 1832.

101   'West View of Lewes Priory' by James Lambert, 1785.

102 St Pancras Priory Ruins, Lewes; postcard in Pelham series, postmarked 16 May 1905. This shows the west end of the second reredorter which now looks less overgrown but is closed behind a chain link fence and gate.

103 A tile from Lewes Priory painted by Gideon Mantell in 1817.

Prior Croham started to receive letters from Thomas Cromwell in 1536, demanding Priory property. On 2 August Croham wrote: 'I have received your letters urging me to make unto you and your assignees, a lease of my manor of Swanburgh'. On 31 August he was again pleading to keep Swanborough, arguing: 'All I have is at the king's command, but I have nothing but the said farm, and grange, and parsonage to maintain my house and hospitality, which, no doubt, it is your pleasure should continue'.

Evidence of unsuitable behaviour was also deemed necessary and in 1535 Dr. Layton obliged by bullying the sub-prior of Lewes into confessing that he had preached treason and the prior knew of it. Croham then had to kneel and grovel. He officially surrendered Lewes and Castle Acre Priory on 16 November 1537. The 23 monks received a cash payment of 40s., and lesser sums were paid to the 80 servants there, starting with John Stempe, the auditor. Three months later

104   St Anne's Church, Lewes.

105   Lewes, St Anne's (formerly St Peter Westout) by Henry Petrie, 1802-06.

Cromwell received the Priory, sold off some of the assets and sent a team of 17 men, headed by Giovanni Portinari, to 'pull down to the ground all the walls of the churches, steeples, cloisters, fraters, dorters, chapterhouses' and the rest.

An outbreak of plague at Lewes in 1538 caused problems in disposing of the bodies of the victims. Thomas Cromwell pressurised the 'honest men' of the parish of St Anne to allow them to be buried in the churchyard, though the adjoining parish of St Michael had been worst hit, and even then they only agreed 'after consultation together for half a day and a night'. St Anne's Church now has a pre-eminent position in Lewes and in 1975 it was one of four livings to be the united benefice of All Saints, St Anne, St Michael and St Thomas, Lewes, now served by the clergy of the team ministry. Lower thought it 'the best of the seven churches of Lewes' but the *St Anne's Church Year Book* for 1947 said: 'St Anne's Church still retains much ancient structural work, although restorations have destroyed much evidence of former interest'.

Lewes had the third largest number of people burnt at the stake in Mary's reign, suggesting that East Sussex was in the forefront of the Protestant Reformation, though a few like the Gages remained true to the old faith. When the Elizabethan settlement finally established the Protestant church, those priests who could not change with the times were deprived of their living. One such was David Michell, formerly a monk of Lewes Priory and later rector of Horsted Keynes: commissioners sent by Bishop Barlow of Chichester reported back on priests who 'are fostered in gentlemen's houses … and are hinderers

106   St Anne's Church, Lewes; postcard by Frith of Reigate.

107   The burning of Richard Woodman and nine other Protestant Martyrs at Lewes on 22 June 1557 in an imaginary street scene.

108   St Thomas à Becket, Cliffe, Lewes postcard.

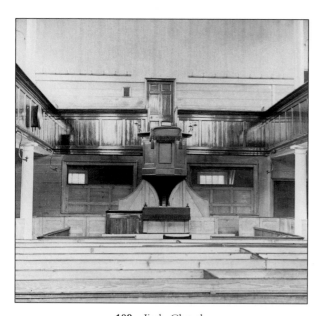

109   Jireh Chapel.

not come to church to be railed at, while others also complained of Huggett's severity towards his family or to parishioners who went to other churches. Huggett was finally removed in 1643 when a Puritan purge in the Civil War deprived eight Sussex clergymen of their livings. In 1635 his church, St Thomas's, had been praised by Dr. Nathaniel Brent on behalf of the Archbishop of Canterbury, particularly the rail round the communion table at St Thomas's which others should copy, as it was 'very comely and decent'.

In 1639 Archbishop Laud confirmed to King Charles that the Bishop of Chichester had certified that everything was well in his diocese except that

> of late there hath happened some little disorder in the east parts of that diocese about Lewes, which we are taking care to settle as well as we can. And for non-conformists, he saith, that diocese is not so much troubled with puritan ministers, as with puritan justices of the peace, of which latter there are store.

Laud did not live long enough to implement his plans and Lewes was left to develop into a melting pot where independence of mind began to emerge, despite external pressure.

In 1660 a petition, signed by Mary Akehurst, Mary Coulstock, Ambrose Galloway the noted Quaker and Mary Dapson, was sent to the justices, warning them that 'the wicked tyrant who is called her husband' had chained Mary in 'a close back-chamber of his house between two high bedsteads with a great chain ... containing 35 links, a staple and a lock'. A copy of this petition was displayed upon the door of St Thomas's Church. Mary Akehurst suffered greatly in her pursuit of truth, perhaps because it caused problems for her husband, a churchwarden, but she survived long enough to win through to worship where she wished.

After the Restoration, different Independent sects emerged, despite the Act of Uniformity in 1662, by which two clerics were ejected from their Lewes churches, the Rev. Edward Newton of St Anne's and Southover, and the Rev. Gwalter Postlethwaite of St Michael's. Both went on to minister to congregations of nonconformists. The rector of Cliffe from 1675 to 1681, William Snatt, was particularly violent against the Quakers, who denounced him in their *Book of Sufferings* as a drunkard, and lover of debauched company, who

of true religion and do not minister. ... Mr. Davy Michell ... frequents Mr. James Gage about Lewes'. In Cliffe, an Irish labourer, Philip Browghowe, proclaimed on 26 April 1600, 'I love not the Queene, nor yet hir lawes, but I love the pope and his lawes with my hart'. The authorities put him in the pillory, with his words written so that all could see his crime, and then he was whipped.

Catholicism was not strong in that period but dissent was gaining a hold. Thomas Prior, a maltster in the Cliffe, was accused of laughing at the parson at Cliffe, Anthony Huggett, and saying that he did

'did keep in his house a Crucifix and other Popish relics'. Alternatively, the Bishop of Chichester, Guy Carleton, wrote to the Archbishop: 'Lewes is so factious a place that the good Mr. Snatt has done is more remarkable'. He was supported by the local JP, Sir Thomas Nut, who fined the non-Anglicans in a variety of ingenious ways from 1670, as recorded by the Rev. Thomas Walker Horsfield, himself a minister at Westgate Chapel from 1817 to 1827. Not all JPs were so biased: Henry Shelley of Lewes was criticised by the authorities for delaying proceedings against the Quakers.

Against this hostile background, the Quakers had begun to gather at the house of John Russell in Southover by 1655, when they were visited by the founder, George Fox, who formed the group into a settled meeting. They was unpopular and had fire or water or dirt thrown at them. In 1673 the Quakers established their first meeting house on Puddle Lane at the bottom of Foundry Lane. Persecution did not stop, as on 15 May 1719 when John Clifton, priest of the Cliffe, demanded two years' tithes, 20 shillings, from Thomas Beard on behalf of the Lewes Quakers. Officers of the parish took from him a silver cup worth about £3, out of which sum only about 13s. was returned. By 1780 the premises needed to be repaired and enlarged, so they decided instead to sell it and build a new Meeting House elsewhere. This went ahead to Friars Walk and the new premises opened in 1784, using a framework of wood hung with mathematical tiles. Their Cliffe meeting house was sold to the new Baptist Church.

On 13 May 1672 the Rev. Edward Newton went to London on behalf of his new congregation to obtain a licence 'for the house of ... Swan, widow, in the town of Lewes, co. Sussex', to be used in the Presbyterian worship of God. In 1676 the pastors of Lewes reported that there were 149 Nonconformists in the region. Thomas Barnard, who worked with Newton before they split, established a congregation at Westgate, also known as Bull Meeting. Barnard was the son of a Lewes draper and could buy the *Bull Inn* and convert the back as a meeting house, seating 400 people. It opened on 5 November 1700 for public worship and over the next sixty years they were joined by other nonconformist groups. Horsfield ministered there from 1817 to 1827, and had imposed conditions before coming to Westgate, including the installation of more comfortable seating and the congregation allowing him to

110 The Rev. Jenkin Jenkins of Jireh Chapel.

engage in 'doctrinal preaching'. For many years Westgate was able to continue because of the generosity of John Every but when he died in 1941 the chapel had to share a minister with Ditchling and later with Brighton. In 1987 the One World Centre opened there and helped to re-establish the chapel financially, so that it can continue for worship.

Bishop Manningham of Chichester in 1718 bemoaned the fact that Lewes was 'miserably overrun with Dissenters', a trend which continued. The Countess of Huntingdon, who was living in Brighton, came to Lewes with Mr. Romaine, a minister, obtaining for him 'one of the pulpits, where his preaching gave great umbrage: he afterwards preached in a large room, and ultimately in open fields'. She therefore built a chapel in Cliffe which opened on 13 August 1765, which started well, but ran into problems.

Nearby was one of the landmarks of modern Lewes, the Jireh Chapel, recently refurbished with help from English Heritage, with an important 19th-century interior. It was 'erected by J. Jenkins, W.A. (Welch Ambassador), with the voluntary contributions of the citizens of Zion, Anno Domini 1805'. Nearby is the burial place of a friend and supporter of Jenkins, the

111   All Saints' Church.

charismatic preacher William Huntington, S.S.
(Sinner Saved), buried on 8 July 1813, whose
epitaph which he dictated calls him the
'Coalheaver, beloved of his God, but abhorred

112   St Michael's Church.

of men'. Sadly, attendances declined and in 1998
the chapel was put in the care of the Rev. Ian
Paisley's Free Presbyterian Church of Ulster, to
maintain doctrinal purity.

In 1807, All Saints was built by Amon Wilds
on the site of an earlier church, 'which had
become so shattered and infirm as no longer to
admit of divine service being performed therein'.
It had united three of the medieval parishes, Holy
Trinity, St Peter the Less and St Nicholas. Further
work to the transepts was done in 1883. When
the church was declared redundant, an imaginative scheme transformed it into a Centre for the
Arts and creative youth activities thanks to a
company known as The All Saints Arts and Youth
Centre (Lewes) Ltd. which came into being in
September 1980.

St Michael's Church had incorporated earlier
parishes, St Martin, St Andrew and St Mary in
Foro about 1546 and has a punning monument to
Sir Nicholas Pelham who died in 1559, aged

113 Repairing the shingles on St Michael's church tower, photographed by Reeves.

forty-four. His successful channel defence gave rise to the couplet:

> What time the French sought to have sack'd Sea-Foord
> This Pelham did repel 'em back aboord.

Its unusual round tower is one of three surviving in Sussex, unlike the main body of the church which by 1748 was said to be so ruinous that parishioners were afraid to attend divine service.

It was rebuilt in 1755 at a cost of about £1,400 and from 1878 the fabric of the building was changed, with Church House added in 1881. In the mid-19th century it was accused of being 'semi-papal', a tradition that persists.

In 1826 Sir Stephen Glynne visited Lewes and found four parish churches in the town, plus those in Cliffe and Southover. He found St Anne's 'a large structure & contains more good work than most of the Churches in Lewes'. He found

114 (Left) Memorial to Sir Nicholas Pelham and his wife Anne in St Michael's Church.

115 (Above) St John sub Castro; postcard.

116 (Below) Eastgate Baptist Chapel, erected in 1843.

117 Eastgate Baptist Chapel to the left and its Sunday School completed in 1893 to the right, photographed by Reeves. This area is now dominated by traffic lights and fast-moving cars.

St John's 'at present a very mean structure having being much curtailed of its original dimensions, and experienced many tasteless modern alterations and mutilations'. He noted in 1846 that 'St John's church has been wholly rebuilt—no trace of the ancient building remains—& the present

church a very ugly quasi-Gothic one with wide sprawling roof & undivided nave'. The building work was done in 1839 by George Cheeseman.

The Independent Tabernacle Chapel opened on 16 November 1816 in the style of a neo-Grecian temple and was enlarged in 1832. Its

118 St Pancras Church.

PROTESTANT MARTYRS' MEMORIAL,
LEWES.

The Committee have great pleasure in informing you that the
FIRST STONE will be laid next WEDNESDAY, OCT. 11TH, 1899,
at 3 p.m., by Captain The Hon. R. BINGHAM, R.N.   His Worship the
MAYOR OF LEWES will preside.

Admission to the Grounds of " Cuilfail " for yourself and friends
on *production of this Card.*

Contributions will be laid on the Stone at the close.

At 5.30 a PUBLIC TEA will be held in the CORN EXCHANGE, Mrs.
ARBUTHNOT and others will deliver short addresses.   Tickets, 6d. each.
Early application requested to Mr. ADDISON, School Hill, Lewes ; Mr.
E. J. MILLER, Pevensey Road, Eastbourne ; or Mr. A. M. ROBINSON,
Rugby Road and Duke Street, Brighton.

At 7.30 a PUBLIC MEETING will be held in the ASSEMBLY HALL.
Chairman, Sir C. R. LIGHTON, Bart.   Speakers : Rev. CHAS. H. H.
WRIGHT, D.D., Rev. A. J BAXTER, Rev. SEYMER E. TERRY, M.A.,
and others.   **Collection.**

If unable to be present, a contribution will be gratefully received by Mr.
GERARD LLOYD, 5, Albion Street, Lewes, Chairman of Committee; or Mr. ARTHUR
MORRIS, 71, North Street, Lewes, Hon. Treasurer.

119 Invitation to the laying of the first stone of the
Martyrs Memorial on 11 October 1899.

IN LOVING MEMORY

of the undernamed seventeen Protestant Martyrs,
who, for their faithful testimony to

GOD'S TRUTH

were, during the Reign of Queen Mary,

BURNED TO DEATH,

in front of the Star Inn—now the Town Hall—Lewes;

THIS OBELISK

PROVIDED BY PUBLIC SUBSCRIPTIONS,

WAS ERECTED A.D. 1901.

	DATES OF MARTYRDOM.
DIRICK CARVER, OF BRIGHTON	JULY 22, 1555.
THOMAS HARLAND, AND JOHN OSWALD, BOTH OF WOODMANCOTE	
THOMAS AVINGTON, AND THOMAS REED, BOTH OF ARDINGLY	JUNE 6, 1556.
THOMAS WOOD (a Minister of the Gospel), OF LEWES	ABOUT
THOMAS MYLES, OF HELLINGLY	JUNE 20, 1556.
RICHARD WOODMAN, AND GEORGE STEVENS, BOTH OF WARBLETON	
ALEXANDER HOSMAN, WILLIAM MAINARD, AND THOMASINA WOOD, ALL OF MAYFIELD	
MARGERY MORRIS, AND JAMES MORRIS (her Son), BOTH OF HEATHFIELD	JUNE 22, 1557.
DENIS BURGES, OF BUXTED	
ANN ASHDON, OF ROTHERFIELD	
MARY GROVES, OF LEWES	

"And they overcame, because of the blood of the
Lamb, and because of the word of their testimony ;
and they loved not their life even unto death."—
Rev. xii. 11. (R.V.)

120 The Martyrs Memorial.

121 The Downs from Cliffe Hill, Lewes; postcard by Valentine, showing the view from the Martyrs Memorial.

congregation included many of Lewes's wealthier residents in the mid-19th century, such as the builder Henry Card and the brewer William Harvey. After a period of disuse, it was finally demolished in July 1955.

On 11 October 1843, Eastgate Chapel, erected by the Baptist church and congregation in this town, was opened, in dismal weather but with a good attendance to hear the sermons from visiting preachers. On the other hand, the Catholics in Lewes had to contend with residual hostility and, when their Chapel was opened on 25 January 1870, a crowd of almost 1,000 had

to be restrained by the police. The unveiling of the Martyrs Memorial on 8 May 1901 caused the 'Lord High Chancellor of Southover' to claim that it was not meant 'as a slap in the face to our fellow Roman Catholic townsmen but as a silent yet speaking, witness for the truth'.

Many Lewes residents will remember when the BBC filmed *Songs of Praise* on 21 October 1989. Unfortunately the weather was not kind but the Gun Garden of the Castle was the venue of a fascinating tribute to the religious diversity of Lewes.

Six

Education in Lewes

Part of the main street of Lewes is known as School Hill, which would indicate a healthy interest in education, except that the name has a completely different root. Paul Dunvan wrote loftily:

> After we have passed the Friars, we enter on the sloping street, called by popular error *School-hill*. That it was originally called by the Saxon inhabitants *Cole-hill, Cool-hill,* will not appear improbable to those who have experienced the constant draught of air that prevails along this street at every season. Vulgar corruption prefixed *S* to the name of this hill.

Suitably chastened, we may prefer L.S. Davey's suggestion that it derives from the fact that its shape resembled a shoe in the early days before its 'instep' was cut away in the 19th century.

Many schools have come and gone in Lewes, too many to mention in detail here, but in medieval times schooling in Lewes was originally a responsibility of the Priory. The monks sent their 'beloved clerk, Lucas, schoolmaster of Lewes' to Rome in 1248 to plead their cause over tithes and John Peckham, who became Archbishop of Canterbury, was educated in Lewes near the priory, as were hundreds of others.

From 1512 there was an alternative, though the Priory was asked to nominate the schoolmaster. A widow, Agnes Morley, endowed a free grammar school in Southover in her will of 1512, to teach grammar at the 'Scolehouse and a garden lying at the Watergate'. To this was added an annuity from his land at Hamsey from another former Lewes pupil, Edmund Dudley, and others such as Thomas Blunt also left money to the Free School. From this the schoolmaster was paid £10 a year and the usher £5. The nine-year-old John Evelyn joined the school in 1630. He had started to learn Latin in 1628 with a Frenchman,

M. Citolin, and from there to 'Mr. Potts in the Cliff; from whom on the 7th of Jan [1630] … I went to the Free-schole at Southover neere the Towne, of which one Agnes Morley had been the Foundresse, and now Edw: Snatt the Master, under whom I remain'd till I was sent to the University.' The Master was a clergyman whose son William Snatt was later to persecute the local Quakers from the Cliffe. Thomas Whalley, the headmaster in the 1680s before becoming rector of St Thomas, Cliffe in 1690, was William Snatt's brother-in-law as both married daughters of the Rev. Thomas Stephenson, rector of St John's, showing that the clerical links remained strong after the Dissolution.

Evelyn also remembered the celebrations for the birth of the Prince of Wales on 29 May 1630, one of many local commemorations about national and royal events. In 1890 when Francis Verrall, younger son of the Lord of the Manor of Southover, married Isabel Thorne of Southover Grange,

> the school children were given presents of tea and buns, and in other ways the event was rendered a memorable one to all concerned, a very pleasant gathering being that of the tradesmen and employees, who dined at the *Swan Inn*, their wives having a meat tea at the *King's Head*.

The tradition survives, as when the Queen and Prince Philip visited Lewes on 16 July 1962, the programme announced that 'children from all the schools in the Borough will line the route from the Malling Down boundary to the Kingston Road boundary'.

In 1709 Mrs Mary Jenkins bequeathed a property on the road up to St Anne's 'to be inhabited and enjoyed by the school-master for the time being of the Free Grammar School in Southover, juxta Lewes, for ever as a free

122 Lewes Grammar School, photograph by Reeves.

donative', plus a sum of money which along with other bequests enabled teaching to continue. The school itself moved to this building in 1714, partly, so it was said, because the master was finding difficulty climbing Keere Street regularly. Paul Dunvan, whose 1795 *History of Lewes and Brighthelmstone* makes such good reading, was an usher at the grammar school for a while. By 1807 the Free Grammar School had 25 boys who were taught classics, reading, writing and arithmetic. Numbers fluctuated, rising to 51 in 1861 under the Rev. Frederick Woolley, but dropping to 23 in 1865. In 1885 the charities were converted into exhibitions which could be held in any place of higher education approved by the governors to boys and girls, children of residents of Lewes or within a five-mile radius. This Lewes Exhibition Fund was administered by 10 governors.

Blaker, looking back in 1919, wrote: 'Of all the changes which have taken place in Lewes during the last few years, not one perhaps has caused deeper regret than the disendowment of the old Grammar School. When I first knew Lewes its reputation stood high, and many of the older men of the present generation received at all events much of their education at that School. The building is now used as a private school.' It was taken over by Thomas Reader White who, according to the *Descriptive Account of Lewes* of 1893, 'conducts it in the most successful manner as a semi-private establishment. This gentleman enjoys the rare distinction, for a school-master, of

having been elected on two occasions Mayor of the Borough, thus showing the high esteem in which educational qualifications are held by the burgesses.' The Old Grammar School still functions from the same building, with a recent advertisement announcing that 'a fully qualified staff encourage hard work, sound learning and good manners'.

Lewes children had several charities to which they could apply. In 1661, for example, the Rev George Steere bequeathed property in Lewes 'for the education and maintenance of a fit person, the son of godly poor parents, especially the son of a godly poor minister, who had truly laboured to win souls unto Jesus Christ, at one of the two universities for the term of four years'.

Otherwise, having wealthy parents helped. The Hon John Byng brought his son to his first school in Lewes in August 1788. 'After Dinner we took our son Henry to the School, seemingly very fit for little Fellows, (kept by Mr. Raymond—a Swiss and his wife, who are very Carefull People, and competent of such Charge) where I hope he will improve in Strength by the goodness of the Air'. This school was the School Hill Academy, founded by Victor Amedée Raymond in 1787, on the site of the *Turk's Head Inn* and demolished in 1821 to build Albion Street. What Byng did not mention was that Raymond required that French 'is the only Language allowed to be spoken among the Scholars, in and out of school hours; Sundays only excepted', though they also studied English, writing, arithmetic and geography, with dancing, music and drawing as extras. Helped by this slightly eccentric education, Henry Byng survived to become a Vice-Admiral.

Raymond was listed as a schoolmaster in the 1793 *Universal British Directory*, as were John Button and Cater Rand, while the Misses Adams ran a boarding school and the Rev W Gwynne was Master of the Free Grammar School. The *Directory* also records under Lewes: 'A charity-school was opened here in 1711, where twenty boys are taught, clothed, and maintained, at the expence of a private gentleman, by whom they were also furnished with books; and eight boys more are taught here at the expence of other gentlemen'.

John Dudeney became one of the characters of Lewes education, coming from a long line of Southdown shepherds, though both parents were literate. They sent him to Dame Mascall, the

123   St Anne's House, home of Mark Antony Lower, *c.*1867. It had once been the home of John Rowe and for a spell was a boarding school; photographed by Reeves.

bailiff's wife at Plumpton Place, but John recorded later that 'all I learnt was how to drive the ducks into the moat, and mother fearful that I might follow them, took me away after a few weeks'. At the age of 10 he met Paul Dunvan who asked to be shown a wheatear's nest and in return gave the child a history of England and *Robinson Crusoe*. The boy became a voracious reader and book buyer, keeping his books and a slate in a hole which he dug while watching his sheep on Newmarket Hill and catching up to 13 dozen wheatears a day, selling them in Brighton for 1s. 6d. a dozen to feed the growing numbers of residents. Dudeney started his first school in Rottingdean and then another in 1804, with 'no other qualification than a real love of learning'. This did not succeed, partly because of the new British School

which began nearby in 1809, but on 26 March 1814 he took over Inskip's evening school at 22 St John's Street. Pupil numbers rose to around 100 and Dudeney also published several text books. He became President of the Lewes Philosophical Society, founded by Brown and Mantell, and was vice president of the new Mechanics Institution. He died in 1852 but his daughter Mary kept up the family tradition by running a school for young ladies at Milton House, Abinger Place.

James Nye, the self-educated poet and gardener, who was born in East Chiltington in 1822, wrote of his education: 'I never went to school but one year and learnt but very little, so that I was almost without learning. But by self practise I learnt to read and write a little,

124 Rotunda of the British School in Lancaster Street, *c.*1898. It was designed in the round so that the teacher could see all the children round him.

which has been a great blessing to me.' In 1858 he became gardener at Ashcombe and came to live in Lewes with his wife and six children, constantly fighting against poverty. In *A small account of my travels through the wilderness*, he wrote that 'the rent and taxes and firing and baking and children's schooling all together came to seven shillings and five pence a week; this left twelve shillings and seven pence per week for eight of us to live on.' His wife and one child fell ill, and 'we was all short of clothes and not a farthing to buy any so my children got so ragged that I could not send them to the school on a Sunday.'

Before compulsory education, and in some instances long after, many rural children probably had similar experiences. As the 19th century progressed, there was more choice for children in Lewes and Lower's *Guide* of 1846 noted that on Lancaster Street, near the House of Correction, stood the British School, 'for boys and girls. It is supported by voluntary contributions, and conducted on the system introduced by the late Joseph Lancaster. The building, which is large and commodious, was erected in 1809. The number of children educated is about three hundred. The school is at all times open to visitors.' The Lewes Little Theatre much later incorporated one of the walls of this building.

While the British Schools operated according to nonconformist principles, the schools of the National Society for the Education of the Poor in the Principles of the Established Church were very different. The National School in Lewes was, according to Lower,

> a handsome building in the Elizabethan style, erected in 1840. The ground-floor is appropriated to boys, and the upper story [*sic*] to girls. The system of instruction adopted is that sanctioned by the National Society, and the building is well adapted to its object. The number of children amounts to about 375. Visitors are admitted at any time, during school-hours. At the lower end of St Mary's Lane, in the immediate vicinity, is an *Infant School* for the children of the poor in connexion with the established church.

The National School building at the corner of what is now Station Street survives, but as a doctors' surgery, and the two figures of charity children, which once adorned it, can be seen at Anne of Cleves House.

There were other options in Lewes for early private schooling. Nathaniel Paine Blaker at eight years old

> was sent to Miss Lee's School, 170, High Street, Lewes, at Christmas, 1843, and remained there one year. Small children in those days generally slept two in a bed, and my bedfellow was William, afterwards Sir William Grantham. ... School life in those days was very different to what it is at the present time, but we were kindly treated and well fed.

Just across Castle Gate, at 166 High Street, Benjamin Abbott ran a school, where 'Sir William Gull, the famous physician, was employed there as an usher. It was said that he first conceived his taste for the study of medicine when nursing one of the pupils through illness', according to the 1893 *Descriptive Account to Lewes*.

Attendance was reasonable. The local paper recorded on 28 June 1890:

> The school attendance at Lewes during the past quarter has been very satisfactory, although not quite up to the average of the corresponding quarter last year. There were 1,656 children on the books, with an average attendance of 1,310, equal to 79.1 per cent. Last year the average was 80.6. St. Anne's is again at the top of the list with the high average of 82.2, the National School being second with 80.

The programme was not wholly dedicated to learning the three Rs and the same paper noted:

> SCHOOL TREAT AT LEWES.—The children attending the St John's Schools had their annual treat on the Racehill, Lewes, on Wednesday. Happily the weather was fine, and there was consequently a goodly gathering of friends and teachers to assist in the sports and amusements provided. There was a bountiful tea, plenty of music, and a large number of prizes and good things distributed. There was a short preliminary service of praise at the church, conducted by the Rector, the Rev. A.P. Perfect.

On 1 April 1903, an Education Committee was formed. It consisted of 12 members of the Corporation and six co-opted members who looked after the eight public elementary schools in the area in 1915. The first on the list was Central on Southover Road, the former National School, for 150 boys and 150 girls, with C.M. Hodges as master, and as mistress. the redoubtable Miss Fowler-Tutt, who was in the vanguard of those keeping Lewes pure from the snares of Rodin's *Kiss*. Next were the junior mixed infants of South Malling, in buildings dating from 1848, followed by mixed and infants at Pells on Pelham Terrace, which opened on 1 February 1897. The *Guide to Lewes* that year by John Sawyer gave an unexpected image: 'As a Voluntary School has been erected as close to the Pells as possible, there are plenty of *al fresco* juvenile dinner parties here in the "prime of Summer time," few schools have such pleasant surroundings'. St Anne's had a junior mixed and infants school, built in 1872 for 142 children and nearby on Western Road was St Anne's mixed, built in 1914 for 160 children. St John the Baptist's, Southover was a junior mixed and infants school, built in 1871, largely at the expense of Miss Laura Verrall, for 182 children and on St John's Street stood St John's School for girls, built in 1871 and catering for 118 children. Finally there was St Pancras School on High Street, for 70 Catholic children.

Older boys could attend the Lewes County Secondary School for Boys which opened on 26 September 1930. The new building was said to be 'worthy of the architecture of the ancient town of Lewes' and was planned to take 300 boys, though 140 started that first day with 100 desks! A quarter were from Lewes and the rest came by bus and train, including 40 from Uckfield whose Grammar School had just closed. Over 50 per cent of the pupils paid fees of £14 a year and the headmaster for the first 30 years was Mr. N.R.J. Bradshaw.

The County Grammar School for Girls had begun in 1913 and, 50 years on, 500 pupils celebrated its jubilee. Merry Tayler of the Upper VIth wrote:

> A visible reminder of the occasion has been added in the form of the wrought iron gates which have been hung at the Grange entrance. May they still be hanging there fifty years hence, when we shall be able to look at them and say (probably to the silent, or otherwise, exasperation of our schoolgirl grandchildren): 'Ah yes, I remember when, in 1963 …'

The gates survive but the schools have changed sites and mixed secondary education continues in the attractive modern buildings of Priory School on Mountfield Road.

Alongside the state schools, Lewes has seen a number of private schools. Elizabeth Bennett's first teaching post, for example, was at 7 Friars Walk, next door to the school run by Mrs. Cripps which she attended, aged 5. In 1932 she moved to Leicester House School, a preparatory school founded the previous year by Miss Salter and Miss Spencer at 2 St Anne's Crescent, partly to cater for children from the Nevill Estate and also the new houses near the Prison. School hours were 9.15 to 12.15 and 12.30 and 2.30 to 3.45 and 4.00, with half days on Wednesdays and Saturdays. During the war, 'schools shared their schoolrooms with evacuees and had many parties to entertain them at Christmas'. The school moved its second home at 54 St Anne's Crescent to a former nursing home in King Henry's Road in 1948. Miss Bennett became head of the Junior School in 1954 after 22 years' service and retired in 1971 from what she found a happy place to work, one of many such smaller educational establishments.

Children could also attend Sunday schools. In February and March 1788, the *Sussex Weekly Advertiser* reported on meetings in Lewes to set up a Sunday school there, or more than one for the various parishes, in the seven parishes of Lewes and Cliffe. Southover had already entered into a subscription for a Sunday school. For the rest, officers were appointed and procedures agreed at a meeting in March where it was resolved:

> That it be recommended, (and it is herein accordingly recommended) to all Ministers, Churchwardens, Overseers, and other Inhabitants of the Town of Lewes, the Cliffe, and Neighbourhood thereof, to open and establish SUNDAY SCHOOLS, within their respective Parishes, for the Instruction of poor Children, of all Denominations.

> That parochial Schools opened as above recommended on proper Application being made to the Secretary, be entitled to the Benefit of the general Fund, raised for the support of this Institution, in such Proportion as their Exigences may require, or as a Committee at their Meeting shall judge proper.

A further mention in the *Sussex Weekly Advertiser,* on 21 December 1789, said that there were two or more operating by this date. By

1846, Lower listed 'Sunday schools in connexion with the following places: St John's church, St. Michael's church, Southover and All Saints churches, Cliffe church, St Anne's Church, the Tabernacle, the Baptist chapel, the Old chapel, with a branch in Southover, the Westgate chapel, and the Westgate meeting'.

Horsfield, who himself ran a school to increase his income whilst at Westgate, wrote:

THE ROYAL LEWES SCHOOL OF INDUSTRY was established February 28th, 1831, under the immediate Patronage of her Majesty Queen Adelaide, in the Parish of Southover, and supported by annual Subscriptions of Half-a-Guinea and upwards, and is open for the reception of boys and girls from the age of six years, under the superintendance of a Master and Mistress. The children are taught reading, writing and arithmetic. The girls are also employed in making and mending their own clothes or those of the subscribers; knitting, or netting, and straw plaiting, and on Friday, in each week, they are taught how to clean a house, and also washing, and making bread. The boys are employed in making baskets … leather boots and shoes which are sold to them at the cost price of the materials; also to clean knives and shoes. The boys are likewise engaged in cultivating a garden which consists of about an acre of ground near the school which they cultivate, and the produce they carry home to their parents. It may be asked what good is likely to be derived from such schools? As we do not intend to enter upon their merits we merely state one advantage which has come to our knowledge, that several of the children on being dismissed from school, instead of playing in the streets, go out to domestic labour in the houses of subscribers, and not only do they work late in the evening, but are willing to rise early in the morning previous to the hour of school; others are allowed to cultivate that portion of ground which has been allotted to them for their own use. The Schools are open every day (Saturday excepted) for public inspection. On the Sunday the children attend those schools and places of worship which their parents prefer.

Modern amateur psychologists might query whether this did not deprive them of their childhood, but it had its uses in creating a useful workforce ready for service.

Girls could also be trained for service elsewhere. In 1826, when her husband William fell from his horse and was killed, Elizabeth Page, née Verrall, opened the Delap Hall Seminary in the Cliffe, in South Street, where she built 'spacious rooms for the reception of a select number of young ladies'. This survived until 1867 when the premises became the Lewes Girls' Home to receive friendless girls to prepare them for domestic service. The need for servants persisted: in 1935, Virginia Woolf noted, 'Went to Lewes, first in the flood, without a rain coat; went to Helen Boyd, two nervous twittering spinsters in a panelled room, about servants: want a 3 day a week girl'. Helen Boyd was an agency at 14 High Street.

Another training opportunity was at East Sussex County Council's School of Domestic Economy at Southdown House, 44 St Anne's Crescent. This had started in Uckfield in 1894 but moved to Lewes in January 1897, with 15 pupils. A special report in 1907 felt that

Southdown House gives a girl training which, followed up, will make her a capable dextrous and sensible woman. She will know one, two or three things well enough to keep her off the rates all her life. Moreover, what is taught at Southdown House is grappling at their source with some of the great national problems and evils such as intemperance (by the agency of good cooking), the proper feeding of the working classes (which affects infant mortality), and the order and comfort of cottage life.

In 1913 the school started to teach cooking to the girls of the new Lewes County Secondary School and two years later it offered to train girls

in plain cookery, laundry work, needlework & household work, & is intended both for girls who wish to go to service & for those who intend living at Home. The course extends over nine months, & the fees vary from 3s. to 5s. a week. Pupils outside the jurisdiction of the East Sussex County Council are also admitted at 8s. a week on certain conditions. Applicants must be of good character, in good health and not under 14 years of age; Miss. M. M. Russell, head mistress.

The war changed the attitude to domestic economy and in 1922 it became a non-residential Domestic Science Centre for girls from the neighbouring schools. This continued until 1937

LEWES MECHANICS' INSTITUTION.

EVENING SCHOOL.

The Members and Friends of the Institution are respectfully informed, that

THE EVENING SCHOOL,

will be reopened on

Monday Sept. 4th.

The Course of Instruction will consist of

Writing, Arithmetic, Grammar, Geography, & History.

The School will be open for Three Evenings in each week, from Seven to Nine o'clock, for Four Months before, and Four Months after Christmas.

The charge for each of these periods of Four Months (or for any shorter time) will be Three Shillings and Sixpence, paid in advance. No other expence will be incurred except for Copy Books.

The Number of Scholars is limited to Thirty, and none will be admitted who cannot read moderately well or who have not had some instruction in writing.

Applications for Admission to be made to Mr. R. Bushell the Secretary of the Institution.

West Street, August 16th 1843.

125 Poster for the new term at the Mechanics' Institution, 4 September 1843.

when the Centre moved to Lewes County Secondary School, leaving their share of Southdown House to the County Library staff, who had started to use it from 1927.

For those in the vanguard of what is now called lifelong learning, there was a Mechanics' Institution in Lewes from 1825, for the purpose of diffusing among the operatives of the town a taste for reading and scientific pursuits. It is far, however, from being limited to mechanics, and its list of members contains the names of many professional gentlemen, merchants, and tradesmen. The building occupies the site of the theatre, and contains a commodious lecture room and a library, with a handsome committee room on the first floor

where the Board of Guardians met weekly. The library held 2,150 volumes and there was also a 'collection of apparatus for philosophical experiments, with a few models, geological experiments, &c.' When Lower wrote this in 1846, there were 190 members. Those in our times who attend WEA or CCE classes, U3A courses or lectures may like to know that the subscription in 1846 was two shillings a quarter which 'entitles members to all the privileges of the institution; and strangers are admitted to the lectures at the very moderate charge of sixpence each'.

The School of Science and Art was built in Albion Street in 1868, at a cost of £2,000, on the site now occupied by the Public Library. Students could follow courses in drawing and painting, etching, geometry, perspective, freehand and model drawing, building construction, designing and modelling, and there were free studentships for a year available to 'artisans and others'. 'This institution is in connection with South Kensington, and has done much to encourage scientific and artistic studies in the town', proclaimed the *Descriptive Account* in 1893. In the 1920s the photographer, E.J. Bedford, became Principal of the Lewes School of Art. The art school closed in 1932 and Bedford became full-time curator of the Lewes Borough Museum which moved in 1934 from the Market Tower to Albion Street. From there he retired in 1950. Lewes Tertiary College provides further education nowadays for A-level courses, evening classes and beyond and is the latest element in the rich tapestry of the town's educational provision.

Seven

Lewes Markets and Fairs

In *A Hand-book for Lewes* in 1846, Lower noted:

> That Lewes has enjoyed the privileges of a market-town for many centuries is certain, although no charter confirming them is extant. The market for corn is held every Tuesday, and that for live-stock on alternate Tuesdays. The business of the former is conducted at the inns, and that of the latter in the High Street. It is to be regretted that a more suitable place is not selected for the purpose. The assemblage of horned cattle, sheep, and pigs in the main thoroughfare of a county-town is surely an inconvenience which requires some better sanction than that of antiquity.
>
> *Clerk of the Market* - W.P. Kell, Esq.
> *Corn Inspector* - Mr. H. Bartlett.
> The annual fairs are four, viz.: on May 6th and Whit Tuesday for cattle; and on Sept. 21st and Oct. 2d. for sheep. The September fair is a very celebrated one, and brings together from 40 to 50 thousand sheep.
> A *wool-fair* is annually held on the 20th of July, and buyers from all parts of the country attend, the South-Down fleeces being held in high esteem.

Across the river in Cliffe the early markets and fairs are better documented and a new plaque on St Thomas's Church Hall records the site of Cliffe's Fair Place. On 12 November 1409 Henry IV granted to his relative Thomas Arundel, Archbishop of Canterbury, permission to hold a market and two fairs in the Cliffe on the feasts of St Mark [25 April] and St Matthew [21 September] and this charter is read out every year as a sonorous opening to Cliffe's Michaelmas Fair. Other markets and fairs had been granted in 1331 and 1345.

The records of the administration of Lewes market begin in earnest in 1564 with a £10 bequest from Mrs. Alice Holter, widow of one of the Fellowship, towards building a new Market-house in Lewes. Fourteen of the Fellowship and Mr. Kyston, commissary for the archdeacon of Lewes, equalled this sum for the benefit of the borough and as a result a new market house was built. The site took over from the earlier one near the church of St Mary in Foro and was in the middle of the High Street, between Castlegate and St Martin's Lane, which was also known as Market Lane for a time. On the map of 1620 it appears as a small circular building with an arcade and its position must have made it hard to ignore. By 1577 clerks were appointed for four markets—for leather, flesh, fish and corn.

Lewes had a corn market by 1630. In 1648, as the reins tightened in local administration as a result of the Civil War, three Lewes men wrote to Lord Dorset, himself a Southover landowner, about continuing the Corn Market in its usual place. Dorset wrote back on 21 December to the noble gentlemen that to put an end to the contest that they mentioned, and as he was himself against innovation, he consented to keeping the Corn Market in its traditional place, which he held to be 'the most convenient for the generalitye of the Towne and Country'. The innovators had their way with the Market House that year, as John Rowe wrote that 'the old markett house was pulled down and the present built 1648'.

Lewes market had the weight of Government legislation on its side, as two 17th-century cases show. In the first John Brockwell petitioned the Council on 30 December 1630 that before the issuing of the Proclamation and Book of Orders [28 September 1630] for restraint of transportation of corn, he

> had bought in Sussex for his own use and supply of his customers, he being a brewer in Lenham, co. Kent, 115 quarters of barley. Complains that the Justices of the County prohibited his bringing the barley to Lenham,

126 Lewes from Cliffe Hill.

127 Lewes, Cliffe by Henry Petrie; sketch showing St Thomas' Church and Cliffe Square, *c*.1803. Petrie drew churches better than horses.

but ordered him to vent the same at Lewes market, co. Sussex, being far remote from Lenham. Prays order that he may transport the barley to Lenham where he lives.

The second case was heard on 16 July 1668 when a jury found that Simon Edmonds of St Thomas, Lewes, 'hath in his possession great quantities of wool without intent to transport the same contrary to an Act of Parliament' of 1639/40. Others were more law-abiding: Thomas Turner noted in his diary for 1 August 1761 that 'in the morn sent my wool to Lewes by John Divol. In the afternoon my brother called on me on his road to Lewes in order to receive both his and my wool money'.

By 1791 the Open Market in Lewes High Street had become a nuisance. The matter went to Parliament and the new Market Bill was passed in May 1791, giving authority to the appointed Commissioners to implement 'An Act for enlarging and extending the present prescriptive Market within the Town and Borough of Lewes in the County of Sussex and removing the same to a more convenient place'. It was agreed not to pull down the present Market House until a new one was in use, so the first meetings concentrated on finding an acceptable site for the new market. After one false start, they agreed that

> the Markett shall be erected on a Spot of Ground the Property of Lord Viscount Hampden adjoining the Crown Inn and yard ... also that a Building be erected in the Front of the said Ground for the purpose of putting therein a Clock and the Town Bell which formerly hung in the Tower of the Broken Church of St Nicholas and that such Clock and Bell be accordingly put up at the time of erecting such Markett.

Work on building the tower was entrusted in the Articles of Agreement of 29 September 1791 to 'Edward May Thomas Standley and Daniel Leggatt all of Lewes in the county of Sussex, Masons and Bricklayers and Amon Wilds George Wille and John Maxfield all of Lewes aforesaid Carpenters'. It was delayed because of a shortage of bricks but on 15 June 1792 the Commissioners were able to announce the new tolls and rules to be observed in the new Market, with summer opening from 1 April to 31 October, from 8a.m. till 4p.m., and from 9a.m. till 3p.m. for the rest of the year. The Lords of the Borough appointed a clerk of the Market to collect

the tolls, out of which the Market Commissioners paid him £5 a year plus five per cent commission on the tolls. The Market Act protected their position, as

> Every person who shall Vend or expose to Sale any manner of Flesh, other raw Victuals Fish Poultry Butter Herbs Roots or Garden Stuff Fruit China Glass and Earthenware out of the Market within the Town and be convicted before two Justices shall for every such offence forfeit 5£ to be levied by distress, 1 Moiety to the Infirm and the other moiety to the Poor of St Peter and St Mary Westout, Saint Michael, St John and All Saints in equal proportions.

From the early days of the Fellowship, Lewes had its own weights, both Troy and avoirdupois, to determine the standard locally. Such weights became very handsome pieces in their own right and found their way into the museum when they became obsolete. Occasionally someone would step out of line and be brought to book for it: for instance, in July 1796 Thomas Verrall of Cliffe, a tallow chandler, was fined 10 shillings for 'having weights used for the Sale of goods not being of the Standard of the Exchequer contrary to the Form of the Statute'.

The autumn sheep fair about 1747 left Cliffe Fair Place and 'removed to a field of Mr. Trayton's and since to a field called the Paddock, belonging to Henry Shelley, Esq., north of the town of Lewes', though the Cliffe people were not happy about the move. Part of the Fair Place then became St Thomas's Square, with houses and a school whose brick footings were probably detected in the excavations of 1987-88. The spring fair, known for its black cattle, continued in the Cliffe and the lower part of Lewes High Street, while pedlary fairs, somewhat similar to modern boot fairs, were still there in the 1830s.

The sheep fair prospered on its new site. The Lewes Journal recorded that on 2 October 1776, 'it was computed that there were 15,000 Sheep at this fair the greatest number ever remembered'. Nine years later,

> the quantity of sheep at the fair was estimated at double the number of last year, which in consequence bore low prices. A lot of 100 fine ewes for which 16/- were refused in the morning, sold at 13s.0d. each. Ewes which sold last year for 20/- sold this for 13s.0d.

By 1805, the *Sussex Directory* by J.V. Button described

> a large sheep fair on the 2nd of October; this fair was formerly kept in the Cliff, but being so much increased, by the celebrity of the Southdown sheep, is held at present (for want of a convenient place in the Cliff), in a field above Shelley's Paddock, and annually draws together from 50,000 to 80,000 sheep; from the bustle and gaiety of the scene, it offers an interesting subject to the pencil of the artist.

Gilbert White had seen the local sheep in 1769 and wrote: 'The sheep about Lewes are all without Horns: & have black faces & legs. Sheep have horns and black faces again west of Bramber'. When William Cobbett came to Lewes in 1822, he wrote: 'I was at Lewes at the beginning of last harvest, and saw the fine farms of the Ellmans, very justly renowned for their improvement of the breed of South-Down sheep'.

In 1813 the Rev. Arthur Young described the Lewes Wool Fair on 26 July:

> This fair was first established in 1786, and the county is indebted to the happy thought which suggested to Lord Sheffield the establishment of such an excellent plan. Before this era, the mode of buying and selling wool was entirely left to chance and uncertainty; and by nobody knowing the fair price, every one sold for what he could get, which necessarily left the seller at the mercy of the stapler; but his Lordship, by instituting this fair, collected the flock-masters together, and a proper price has ever since been obtained.

This idea soon took hold in East Anglia, too.

In the four years from 1809 to 1812 there were reports addressed to the Wool-Meetings at Lewes 'On the Trade in Wool and Woollens, including An Exposition of the Commercial Situation of the British Empire' by the President, John, Lord Sheffield, from the Communications to the Board of Agriculture. In 1810, for example, it was disclosed that 'the same backwardness to purchase which took place at Lewes, prevailed at other wool fairs', as English wool prices had dropped, though elsewhere the prices of Southdown wool rose and had improved in quality.

The Board of Agriculture's report on *The Agricultural State of the Kingdom* in 1816 moni-

128 Portrait of John Ellman (1753-1832).

tored the drop in the previous two years from prosperity to extreme depression and John Ellman junior confirmed that

> in many instances in this neighbourhood [Lewes] strong able men, from the want of other work, are employed in picking stones, &c., which would otherwise be done by women and children, for whom no employment can now be found. I consider the distress of the farmers so great, that nothing can be done to save many from absolute ruin.

This problem was still causing concern when William Cobbett supported the Sussex labourers at a meeting in Lewes on 9 January 1822, though the Sussex farmers tried to stop him speaking because of his criticisms of them the previous year, and he reminded the landowners that they owed everything to their labourers. Discontent was still simmering in 1830 when the Captain Swing riots gathered momentum and the riot leaders at Ringmer asked:

> Have we no reason to complain that we have been obliged for so long a period to go to our daily toil with only potatoes in our satchels, and the only beverage to assuage

129 A View from Baxter's Library, High Street, School Hill, Lewes, sketched by Thomas Herwood on the day of the Ascent by Mr. Green & W.H. Gardiner Esq., 29 September 1828.

our thirst the cold spring; and on returning to our cottages to be welcomed by the meagre and half-famished off-springs of our toil-worn bodies?

It was against this uneasy background that the Lewes Fairs took place and on 21 September 1846, for instance, Charles Wille went to the Lewes Fair Day, but found 'about half the number of sheep pen'd as is usual'.

Lewes Sheep Fair in 1809 was moved from its normal date of 2 October to 21 September, as Croydon had adopted the former date. This gives some idea of the wide catchment area for the fairs, which also provided a good opportunity to show off in front of a large crowd. In 1828 Henry

Green did just that, making an ascent in his balloon in front of 15,000 people, of whom 10,000 were watching from Cliffe Hill. The conditions were not ideal and his passenger had to step down from the basket to allow Green to get off the ground at all. He managed to stay up in the balloon for 45 minutes before landing in a field at Deanlands Wood, near Ripe. He returned to Lewes to make an appearance at the Public Temple, the local theatre, where he described his voyage to admiring cheers from the audience. A different ascent ten years later by Charles Green and Charles Rush baffled the Southover farmer in whose field the balloon landed on 10 September 1838. He came past to find the inflated balloon

130 Site of the Livestock Market, with the *White Hart* in the background, photographed by Reeves.

131 Sheep filling most of the High Street outside St Michael's Church, watched by John Every from his car, *c.*1910, and photographed by Reeves.

surrounded by hundreds of interested spectators and hurried over to Green saying: 'How'd ye come here? Why didn't you send word? I'd have left the gate open rather than ye should broke down the hedges'. He was placated by the offer of half a sovereign.

The Rev. Arthur Young wrote in 1813 that the Lewes Sheep Fair

> is annually held upon the second day of October; and it is from hence that the South Down flocks are dispersed over various quarters of England, as the buyers come from a great distance to attend Lewes upon this day, where large droves are bought up by commissions. From 20 to 30,000 sheep are generally collected upon this occasion.
>
> Previous to this fair, there is one at Selmiston (September 19) upon a much smaller scale. But the principal flocks are drafted and sold previous to either of these fairs, so that a buyer who comes from another county, and examines the sheep upon the day of the fair, is deprived of seeing the finest part of this celebrated stock.

Lewes Annual Horse Fair was first held on 30 August 1832, with what Horsfield described as 'a very good shew of Stock, and the company numerous'. Horses had an important part to play in the life of Lewes, both as working animals or means of transport or as mounts for hunting or the stars of Lewes Races. In 1793 the *Universal British Directory* wrote of Lewes:

> Between this town and the sea, there is the best winter-game that can be had for a gun, and several gentlemen here keep packs of dogs; but the hills hereabouts are so steep, that it is extremely dangerous to follow them, though their horses will naturally run down a precipice safely with a bold and skilful rider.

Nathaniel Paine Blaker reminisced about the Lewes of his childhood from 1843 when

> a cattle-market was held in the Town on alternate Tuesdays, and pens formed of oak wattles for sheep extended from the '*White Hart Hotel*' for some distance towards St Michael's Church and occupied a considerable part of the road. Besides the sheep there were numbers of bullocks and horses, and these, together with the sheep, took up a great part of the width of the road and interfered a good deal with the traffic.

This had begun in 1789 when Lewes people resolved that a market for live-stock twice a month would be for the general good of the town, though a Whit Tuesday cattle fair existed for 90 years from 1744. There was also a Sussex Cattle Show which on 9 July 1858 was held in the Priory grounds.

The *Sussex Advertiser* of 28 September 1847 reported: 'Extra trains from the Lewes Station proceeded on the Keymer Branch to the junction with the London line at Haywards Heath, instead of going round by Brighton. A great number of sheep from Lewes fair was also forwarded via the same branch on Tuesday'. Although most fairs passed without incident, this was not always the case, and Wille was on hand at the Lewes Sheep Fair on 21 September 1859 where 'the Engine of Cheal's Threshing Machine burst & killed several men & a Gentn. & his horse, on which he sat, with 5 sheep near'.

The shepherd Len Tuppen recalled his time at Houndean when

> we used to go to the annual Lewes Sheep Fair which was held on the Old Fair Ground, just north of Lewes Prison. The Michaelmas Fair was always held in September; thousands of sheep were driven from far and wide. Thornton's were the auctioneers—Mr Redman used to sell all the ewes while Mr Profit White sold the rams. ... As the fair was held on land which was part of Houndean Farm, Richard Brown was responsible for collecting the wattles from the surrounding farms to form the sheep pens.

Mr Brown sold his 800 acres of Houndean in 1928, selling everything at the Sheep Fair from milking pails to old horses, and his pure bred Southdown flock of 445 ewes and ewe lambs which had started in 1901.

In 1879 the Lewes Cattle Market Company was incorporated by a Special Act of Parliament for

> the purpose of establishing a Market, or Markets, within certain limits which comprise an area of two mile radius from the County Hall at Lewes, for the Sale of Cattle, with Market Places and Market Houses, and all requisite Buildings, Stables, Sheds, Slaughter House, Approaches and other works and conveniences; and for that purpose to hold and use any Land vested in the Company by the Act, and from time to

132 Lewes Sheep Fair, *c.*1891, photographed by Bedford.

133 Lewes Sheep Fair: 'Striking a Bargain', photographed by Bedford.

134   Poster advertising a public meeting to discuss the removal to a new site of the Cattle Market, 22 January 1878.

135 Harvesting at Houndean Rise, 1901, photographed by J.A. Sharpe. The hedge and trees on the skyline marked the side of Juggs Road and the wooden bar fence was the division between the fields and the Brighton-Lewes Road.

time to purchase, but by Agreement only, and hold any other Lands not exceeding in the whole seven acres which they may require for any of the purposes aforesaid. The Company are empowered to purchase, or take on Lease, additional Lands, not exceeding ten acres, for the purpose of depasturing cattle. The Act of Parliament empowers the Company to demand and take tolls from persons using the market, and further imposes a restriction against any person selling or offering Stock within the radius of two miles from the County Hall, except in Market Place, under a penalty of Five Pounds, which practically secures the Company from any opposition.

This new fortnightly market was held on Wood-cock Field, part of St John's Farm, behind what became St John's Terrace. The new borough of 1881 expressed concern about the sanitary aspects

of this new site and opened negotiations to transfer to the Corporation the market privileges given them by their Private Act. Their Committee eventually rejected the plan to spend £800 on buying these market privileges but encouraged the move to a new site, the old Tanyard, with the lease of a garden near the railway station. Tanning had been an important industry in old Lewes, using bark from the Weald, and pervading the town with its smell, but it became unprofitable and died out here and at Malling.

The Lewes Cattle Market Company bought this site for £4,000 and in the prospectus of 23 May 1883 potential shareholders were offered the chance to buy 300 of the 400 shares at £10 each, payable to the General Manager, auctioneer Ebenezer Wells, or the Secretary, H.J. Bartlett, at the Company's registered offices at 19 Station Street. On 26 June 1883 the market

136–8 Three photographs by Fred Marzillius of the demolition of the Cattle Market in 1994–5.

started as a weekly open market in this new location where the premises were 'paved, drained and fitted, to meet the requirements of the Privy Council and the Local Sanitary Authorities'. The Lewes Fatstock Show moved to this new site as well, away from its original base on Albion Street. There was a plan that the Corn Market, which had been held in the Exchange for many years, should also move to the new site, but the Corporation was against this, recognising the importance of a Corn Market to an agricultural town like Lewes. In 1890 the Corporation decided instead to renovate the Corn Exchange in its existing site and improve the facilities around it, adding a Public Assembly Room. It ended up on the east of the new Town Hall which was completed in 1893.

John Sawyer's *Guide to Lewes* in 1897 reported:

> Near the Station is a Cattle Market, which does not seem to do an extensive trade, but whether this is due to the establishment of rival markets, or to the importation of frozen meat, this deponent cannot say. The business at the Corn Exchange (market every Tuesday) is by sample. The room appears to be run by a Company, and 2d. must be paid and a ticket taken by each visitor who from any cause wishes to pass the turnstile.

Market day was part of everyday life. Elizabeth Bennett remembered her childhood in early 20th-century Cliffe:

> Every Monday was market day and early in the morning flocks of sheep and herds of cows were driven up the Cliffe over the bridge round to Friars Walk, Lansdowne Road, Southover Road, leading to Garden Street, the site of Lewes Cattle Market. After the cattle were sold, the auctioneer proceeded to a large building filled with plants, crockery, tools, furniture, beds, books, and odd lots, which were auctioned. Afterwards the owners of the various goods queued at the office to receive cash due. The market was crowded with farmers and many onlookers. Mr. Turnbull the vet was actively employed during the day. After his house was another butcher, who did a good trade.

The Cattle Market closed in 1992 with its buildings remaining as a sad reminder of former times until demolished to make room for new houses, on either side of a street with the new name of Tanners Brook. The traditional Fatstock Dinner was revived in 1993 as the County Town Dinner & Fatstock Celebration by Lewes Round Table, itself one of the oldest Tables at No. 37. It keeps alive the old traditions in awarding farming prizes, as well as creating new ones with the award to the Lewes Personality of the Year.

Eight

Law and Order

In 1969 there were proposals in Lord Beeching's Royal Commissions that Assize and Quarter Sessions should move from Lewes to Crawley. One journalist, known as 'South Saxon', responded: 'To innocents not versed in the law it may seem strange that Lewes is so angry. It may also seem perverse that it is so proud that for over 700 years it has seen more poor devils sentenced for treason, murders and felonies than any other Sussex town.'

The move did not succeed, though there was a break in the 1990s when the County Court was refurbished, but Lewes's assize tradition goes back to Edward I's reign and catered for a range of crimes. In July 1730, for instance, the *Sussex Advertiser* recorded: 'On Monday the Assizes ended at Lewes for the County of Sussex, when one Person, Richard Eldridge, was convicted capitally for horse-stealing; two were burnt in the Hand, but none were order'd for Transportation.'

In 1749 Lewes formally became the Assize Town for the whole of Sussex, with a new sessions house to replace the old wooden one in 1761. This in turn was replaced by a new Shire Hall or Sessions House on High Street, built at a cost of £25,000 in Portland stone by John Johnston over the period 1808-1812, and topped by panels of Coade stone representing Wisdom, Justice and Mercy. It survives today as the County Court, the scene of many notable trials, drawing the crowds. Mrs. Dudeney recorded one such occasion on 19 July 1924 when the Bungalow murderer Patrick Mahon was found guilty of killing Emily Kaye:

> Horrible excitement in the town about the Mahon trial. The most ghoulish touch was the crowd in Castle Ditch, a spot always deserted. I came home that way as a short cut, being late for lunch. The gates leading to the Assize Court well back, a covered grey motor lurking there, guarded by bobbies, waiting to take the prisoner back.

Lewes Castle had acted as a prison, often for a short stay before the prisoner was sent on to Guildford. The name of 'Hamelin the Porter of Lewes who holds the prison in fee' survives from 1278 and the town may have had its own facilities. In 1487 the inhabitants of Sussex petitioned for a jail to be erected 'at a place convenient within the town of Lewes', as Guildford was too far. The martyrs in Mary's reign occupied the prison vaults under the *Star Inn*, but in 1576-7 the Town Book records that the new constables received, amongst other adjuncts to their offices, 'one Locke of the weste gate wyth ii kayes whiche gate & house are the prisons for the towne'. Cliffe had a new House of Correction in 1610 and this survived unchallenged until 1793.

Crimes were variable. Amongst the collection of petitions in Charles I's reign is:

> Petition of Robert Gouldham, butcher, late of Cliffe, Sussex. That being troubled for tithes by Mr. Hugget, minister of Cliffe, he was obliged to pay into court 26s. 8d. although the tithes of the tenement he then occupied had previously been paid by his landlady. He has remained in prison there 20 months, where he is ready to perish for want, unless your Worship cause Mr. Hugget and his proctor to make restitution of the money received by them, and so long wrongfully retained.

Hanging was the penalty for many offences and the town gallows were said to have been on the site later filled by the *Elephant and Castle*, though Horsfield reckoned that the site was within Hangman's Acre, about 100 yards south west of the pub.

139   Lewes Naval Prison, which began life as the House of Correction in 1793.

The House of Correction at the corner of North Street and Lancaster Street was built by James Fentiman of Stoke Newington and opened in 1793, to what Horsfield described as 'the plan recommended by the benevolent Howard', the great prison reformer. The *Lewes Journal* of 7 December 1782 had noted that 'the celebrated Mr. Howard visited the House of Correction in the Cliff', which had catered for residents of the Rapes of Lewes and Pevensey and closed as this new one opened.

In 1817 the House of Correction was extended, 'with a view to more perfect classification of the prisoners', as Horsfield noted. Its treadwheel worked a mill in the prison and more fortunate prisoners were soon able to work in the new manufactory for mops and mats. In 1833 there were three Houses of Correction in Sussex, at Petworth, Lewes and Battle, plus Horsham Gaol. At Lewes the Keeper was paid £170 a

year, the chaplain £200 a year with a minimum duty of four hours, a surgeon four shillings per head for every prisoner committed and the matron £40 a year, all four being appointed by the magistrates. They were backed by a taskmaster and turnkeys, four male and one female, all appointed by the Keeper. At this period the Keeper was Thomas Ancell who told the commissioners that the boundary wall of the prison had been greatly extended in 1834 with a new wing for female prisoners, entirely separate from the male prison. 'A new Chapel has also been built, capable of containing 200 Prisoners with proper kneeling Places, and a Gallery for Magistrates'.

Some idea of how the system operated comes from the *Reports from Committees on Gaols and Houses of Correction* in 1835. Sixteen of the potential complement of 134 prisoners were questioned, the youngest being 13, and their complaints noted. Their crimes varied from passing counterfeit coin

140 'Russian Prisoners at Lewes from Life.'

to poaching to housebreaking, and another was 'committed before for making a Row at the Fair in December 1833, and also about Four Years ago for a Row at a Public House'. One said that if he were to live that time again, he 'would rather be shut up solitary than exposed to the bad Conversation of the Day-rooms'. Another 'could neither read or write, had only learnt a little Spelling since in Prison'. A third felt he was 'a much better Man since he has had the Allowance of Potatoes (given after three months)', while others thought the food was better than Petworth.

When Horsham Gaol closed, Lewes provided the County Gaol for the Eastern division of Sussex. By 1850 it was recognised that the prison was too small, as the committals in east Sussex had increased in the years from 1830 to 1850, so the county began building a new gaol. This, the present Lewes prison, was built by D.R. Hill of Birmingham and was first occupied in 1853.

At the start of the Crimean War, in June 1854 a government surveyor came to Lewes to see if the House of Correction would be suitable as a base for Crimean prisoners of war. He found it was, but agreed that soldiers should be stationed in the town to protect the locals. The government bought the gaol for £5,000 and by August alterations were in hand, with Mr. Card the builder and Messrs Diplock, plumbers, using a team of 200 men. A month later, the *Brighton Gazette* reported:

> 300 men are now employed on the work. The gas has been laid on and all parts of the building are well lit. Mr. Morris, an ironmonger of the Cliffe, is employed on this work and has a number of fitters at work. The wall facing North Street has been lowered several feet.

The first consignment of 150 prisoners arrived on 5 October and were made

141 St John's Church, Lewes; postcard showing the memorial to the Russian prisoners of war.

as comfortable as possible and are said to like their food amazingly. They have taken up manufacturing puzzles and other toys in wood, which they dispose of to visitors (freely admitted) and to shops in the town and in Brighton. Each cell (three to a cell) has a copy of the Scriptures, and they are about to get a Russian speaking chaplain.

Not all were Russian, as the Swedes and Finns were enmeshed in the same conflict, but during their enforced stay in Lewes they were treated with considerable leniency. At the funeral of one Finnish prisoner, on 27 March 1855, Wille wrote that 'first the English service was perform'd in & out the Church, after which one of the Fins read a Service & then sung a Hymn'. Escapes took place, with a few brave men risking a 12-foot drop from the roof of the guard house to the street, though one was 'shortly afterwards discovered in the *King's Arms*, a public house not far

from the prison, where he had just purchased a half pint of rum'.

When the war with Russia ended in 1856, the prisoners and their captors parted on good terms. The 326 prisoners departed in late April, accompanied by the Lewes Saxon Horn Band and the Governor of the Military Prison, Lieutenant Mann, and crowds of townsfolk to wish them well. Twenty-eight prisoners had died in the gaol, mainly from pneumonia, and their names are recorded in the churchyard of St John sub Castro on the memorial erected by Tsar Alexander II in 1877, and restored by the Russian Embassy in 1957.

As many thought

this Ancient County Town should be honoured with some Russian Trophy application was made in October last by the Chief Officers of the Borough supported by the Borough Members to Lord Panmure

142 The memorial in the churchyard of St John sub Castro.

143 The inscription on the memorial to the Russian prisoners of war.

who was at that time Secretary of State for War expressing a hope that his Lordship would be pleased to present this Town with a Russian Gun to be preserved as a Trophy of the late War and calling his Lordship's attention to the Fact that about 300 Russian War prisoners were confined here during the late War.

Lord Panmure agreed and presented Lewes with 'a Russian gun which was taken in the late War', for which he had 'a Russian Gun Carriage Manufactured for it at the Royal Arsenal at Woolwich'. The gun and its carriage arrived in June 1858, to be installed in the castle grounds, where it has been on view in different locations ever since.

Nathaniel Paine Blaker worked at the Naval Prison as Assistant Surgeon in 1859:

There were about 300 invalid convicts, of who about 20 or 30 were mental cases, some bordering on insanity; a considerable number were convalescents after accidents or acute disease, sent from able-bodied prisons, and some were chronic invalids. We remained at Lewes four or five months, when we were transferred to a newly-built model prison at Knapp Hill, close to Woking.

Miss Bennett recalled that, before the First World War, Mr. Bray lived on Morris Road and was a warder at the Naval Prison,

where seamen served their sentences and afterwards he escorted them back to Portsmouth by train. He was a kind man and each time borrowed Robert's Gladstone bag and filled it with bread and cheese for the sailors and himself on the journey. The

144   N.E.S. Norris and L.F. Salzman of the Sussex Archaeological Society visiting the Naval Prison before demolition in 1963.

naval authorities also owned Admiralty House, a large convalescent home for naval officers in Wallends Crescent.

In 1914 all the prisoners were returned to Portsmouth where the sailors were put to work on various boats. 'Now the prison was taken over by the army and officers in charge of training, also a sergeant who was instructor for physical exercises.' As the war progressed, the troops moved away and both the Naval Prison and Lewes Prison were used to house prisoners of war.

Help was scarce and farmers employed them to work on their farms. Each day in the week German prisoners would be escorted in little bands to various places in the area to work where needed, some looking after the animals on the farm, planting, harvesting or clearing river banks or ditches. Others worked in the factories.

The Naval Prison was home to the Territorial Army for a while but on 1 September 1939 they

left it and the Drill Hall in an army transport to prepare for war. It again housed prisoners of war, as did Southease, and they worked hard on local farms. At Christmas 1945 an appeal was made for local people to invite them to their homes on Christmas Day and the response was good. This imposing building was demolished in 1963, though not before two representatives of the Sussex Archaeological Society had visited the site and acquired as a memento a prison door which is now on display at Anne of Cleves House.

On the Brighton Road to the west of Lewes, the County Gaol was extended in 1868 and continued as a prison until 1917 when it closed for 14 years. It then reopened as a local prison and from 1949 also included a young prisoner centre, though this stopped in 1964. A bad fire in 1968 led to the living accommodation being rebuilt to a high standard. It then housed 280 adult prisoners, mostly serving sentences from 18 months to four years, and was a training prison. Latterly it has housed a local remand wing, a remand wing

145 A view of the interior of the Naval Prison in 1963, showing one of the doors which was acquired for display at Anne of Cleves House. (Reproduced by kind permission of the Sussex Archaeological Society.)

for teenagers awaiting appearance in London courts and the traditional accommodation for prisoners, with up to 440 men at any one time, though the design was for 300 prisoners.

In its time, Lewes Prison has seen a range of inmates. Wille recorded on 2 May 1860: 'Mr. Hopley committed to Lewes Prison for slaying &c. one of his pupils'. Hopley, who ran a school in Eastbourne, had flogged a pupil, Reginald Chancellor, so severely that the boy died. In 1868 Wille recorded 'the Man for the Murder on the Hill near Kingstone brought to Lewes'. This was Martin Brown who had shot a shepherd named Baldy. On 18 January 1869, he was hanged for this murder, in the first execution at Lewes conducted privately.

One famous prisoner at Lewes was Eamon de Valera, who was transferred there at the end of 1916. Lewes was known for better conditions than other gaols and the removal to Lewes of this important political prisoner with other Irishmen was partly an attempt to placate Irish American

opinion. De Valera started to organise his fellow prisoners very effectively and there were rumours of an escape plan which involved two young Irish undergraduates enticing the guards away from their posts so that de Valera could escape. This imaginative scheme did not come to fruition and after a few months at Lewes he was returned to Maidstone, a curious career path for the first President of the Irish Republic.

Prison was only one element of the protection of its citizens. *Much Ado about Nothing* gives some idea of the somewhat chaotic forces of law and order from Tudor times. High Constables were appointed for a year for each hundred and Petty Constables for each parish, and could pay a fine or hire a substitute. In 1837 the Borough of Lewes acted under the Lighting and Watching Act of 1837 and appointed four paid full-time watchmen, Ballard, Harmer, Kennard and Burridge, who were known as the Town Watch. Down the road, Charles Wille's diary

146   Lewes Prison, with a corn field in the foreground on the opposite side of the Brighton Road; from a glass negative.

for 7 August 1838 has the entry: 'Attended Commissioners Meeting to take into consideration the propriety of establishing Police in the Cliffe'.

In 1840 the East Sussex Constabulary came into being with the swearing in on 8 December of a force consisting of the Chief Constable, Captain Henry Fowler Mackay, and 15 men, including the four watchmen from Lewes, of whom Ballard was the sergeant and the other three constables for the Lewes district of seven parishes. The regulars worked alongside 120 local constables in the county. The yard of the old *Star Inn*, which was occupied by the town fire engine house, had two cells used by the old Town Watch and their successors, the new constabulary.

In 1842 Henry Card built a new police house in Lancaster Street, at a cost of £198 2s. 0d. and in 1846 it became the County Police Headquarters. The service was paid for by residents, as on 3 January 1843 when Wille 'attended Quarter Sessions, & paid County & Police rate'. The Sussex police force gradually established themselves under the watchful eye of Captain Mackay who

retired in 1881, aged 79. A farewell parade was held at the Dripping Pan when nine superintendents, 15 sergeants and 65 constables were on parade.

On 25 March 1884 the police took over their new purpose-built headquarters and Divisional station at the corner of West Street and St John Street, in what came to be the Lewes Police Station. Many were detained in the cells there over the years, including a disorientated German pilot in World War II who was carrying mail between the Channel Islands and Cherbourg, but landed on the Race Hill in the fog, thinking it was France. In 1948 the headquarters of the reformed East Sussex Force moved to Malling House on Church Lane, which became the headquarters of the Sussex constabulary when the five constituent forces combined on 1 January 1968, and the original team of 15 had expanded to over 3,000 in the new style Sussex Police. Lewes Police Station became the administrative headquarters for policing the Lewes area and the fine red brick building celebrated its centenary in 1984.

147 Funeral of the late Supt. Stevens, 24.4.1909, postcard. The funeral procession of this well respected policeman is making its way down Cliffe High Street.

148 Police Superintendents, 23 June 1881 at the presentation to Lt. Col. Mackay:
Front row, left to right (with years of service): Supt. George Berry, 16 years, Supt. William Pocock, 37, Supt and Dep. Chief Constable William Waghorn, 35, Supt James Jenner, 35, ?.
Back row: ?, ?, Supt. John Pearless, 35, Supt. Thomas Osbon, 26, Albert Waghorn, Chief Clerk, 3. Photographed by Reeves.

Nine

Health

Lewes had facilities to cater for those in need and many Lewesians left bequests to distribute food and money to the poor. The Old Poor House of St John's on Castle Banks was built in 1633. In 1835 its function as a Workhouse ceased and it became the *Travellers Rest*. In 1927 the building was bought by Mrs Dudeney, who found cleaning it 'too exciting for words. I must get to work and make money to pay for all this delirious fun. I did work quite nicely and I was so happy in a sleek, whisker-washing way all day long.'

Wille's diary for 4 November 1840 recorded: 'Met the Churchwardens and overseers respecting the new building for the Union house, Cliffe'. On 12 March he 'attended Board, went to St Ann's & All Saints Union house, was detained till 4 o'clock.' The background to this was that Lewes Union comprised all seven parishes, with 11 Guardians, and Lower recorded in 1846:

149 The old Lewes Workhouse, photographed by Reeves.

No general poor-house has been established, but the old parochial houses have been appropriated to the purposes of the Union. The able-bodied paupers occupy the poorhouse of the Cliffe, the aged poor that of All Saints, and the children that of St Anne's. The number of persons who received relief last year was 1268, and the number admitted to the poor-houses, 181.

A workhouse was erected in 1868 in de Montfort Road but demolished and replaced in 1960 by municipal flats.

The Dissolution had removed Lewes Priory's influence in education and health. The monks had been cared for in the Priory's Infirmary, though sometimes the illness was beyond care, as when the Black Death, which began in 1348, took its heavy toll in Lewes as elsewhere. Their foundation of St James's Hospital in Southover had helped local people to cope with health problems, as had St Nicholas's Hospital on Western Road. Dunvan, writing in 1795, noted that St Nicholas Westout was near the site of the Battle of Lewes, when

> most of the slain on that day were interred in pits in the field or croft adjoining the hospital; and a few years ago, as they were making the new turnpike road from *Lewes* to *Brighthelmston* through this parish, the workmen dug into one of those pits, and threw up a great quantity of human bones.

Excavations in the 1990s confirmed this.

Poverty often causes health problems and removes solutions. James Nye wrote of his time in Lewes in 1859 when his eldest boy fell ill and 'was forced to have a doctor. … He has been in bed ever since, which is over three years. With the boy's earnings we was going to pay our debts, but his money was stopped at once'. His three shillings a week had been crucial to the family's survival. Friends were very generous and helped to meet some of the expenses, though the doctor's bill exceeded four pounds. 'The doctor thought it best to send the poor boy to the hospital. And he went and lay there seven months and then came home incurable. While he lay there my wife was confined by the eighth child'. Nye's daughter found a job in Brighton to help to pay the bills but 'sunk into a galloping consumption' which took three months to kill her. It must have been immensely difficult for men like Nye to hang on to their self respect and

faith, but he survived as a Calvinist, musician and instrument maker and poet on top of his working life as a gardener.

There was some official help. Lower described the Benevolent Society which was formed in 1794:

> Its object is the relief of the sick poor of every religious creed. Visitors are appointed in monthly rotation to carry into effect the objects of the institution, by paying visits to the necessitous, and affording them a small pecuniary aid. The funds are raised by subscriptions, donations, and sermons preached at the Old and Baptist chapels.

At the same time there was a Dorcas Society, which 'conducted by a committee of ladies, was established for the purpose of supplying clothing to the necessitous, and it deserves the increased support of the affluent'.

Though Lewes could not benefit as it was inland, the popularity of the Sussex seaside towns developed from the work of a Lewes doctor. Dr Richard Russell, son of another Lewes medical man, Nathaniel Russell, owned 77-79 High Street and attended St Michael's Church. In a book of 1752 which he dedicated to the Duke of Newcastle, he praised the effects of sea water to cure tuberculous glands. His idea was that the sea water should be drunk, as the salts were beneficial, but most patients felt that bathing in it was preferable and so Dr. Brighton was born and the seaside became fashionable. Russell attended Thomas Turner's pregnant wife in 1754 but Turner usually went to Dr. John Snelling of Lewes and Alfriston, who indulged his enthusiasm for blood letting, as in 1756 when the doctor opened 'one of the capillary arteries of my temple for the benefit of my eyes'. Previously he had recommended 'a poultice of conserve of roses, and about 6 gr. of champire in each poultice, to be laid to my eye, with purging twice a week with sal. glabuler and manna'.

Perhaps the most famous doctor in Lewes was Gideon Mantell. He was born in 1790, the son of a Whig shoemaker. He went to a dame's school and then to Mr Button's school in the Cliffe, as his father's principles excluded him from the Grammar School. After further schooling in Wiltshire, he was apprenticed to Dr. James Moore, a Lewes surgeon, who from 1815 lived at one of the houses now 165-167 High Street. They were built by Amon Wilds about three years earlier on the site of the *White Horse Inn* and were known as Castle Place. Mantell bought the central houses in 1819 and is probably responsible for the front being plastered and the ammonite columns added. The house, recently renovated, is the base of the Guild of Master Craftsmen.

Dr. Mantell became a partner in the practice when he finished his medical training, specialising in midwifery, but also saving a woman accused of poisoning her husband by proving that the medical tests for arsenic were untrustworthy. He loved his native town and was fascinated by anything from antiquity to natural history and geology, growing in stature nationally by his work on the iguanodon remains that his wife found in Tilgate Forest while he was attending to a patient. Though he moved away, he came back to Lewes regularly to check progress and see old friends. One such case took place on 20 October 1849 when he came back by train from London to see George Grantham's father, but arrived at his bedside in time to exchange a few words, thanks to 'a mismanaged case of pericarditis brought on by other fatigue in shooting three weeks ago'. Mantell became an honorary fellow of the Royal College of Surgeons in 1844 and died in 1852, after a long-term spinal problem.

In January 1795 Lewes residents were threatened when smallpox broke out at the home of George Apted in St Mary's Lane and he refused to have his infected children removed. Dr. Thomas Frewen, a physician in Lewes, had written on *The Practice and Theory of Inoculation* for smallpox from 1749, so the groundwork was in place, though Edmund Jenner's work did not start in earnest until 1796. Dunvan recorded that nearly 3,000 were inoculated in a 'plan of General Inoculation' and only about 45 died as a result, which was felt to be acceptable. Those inoculated ranged in age from over 80 years old to eight hours, a baby being inoculated successfully by the surgeon Henry Verrall.

Dunvan suggested as a result that a suitable inoculating house should be built 'in any of the retired *combs* or vales in the vicinity of the town' with a skilful surgeon and 'sober and industrious nurses'. In fact Lewes had such provision from 1742 when an isolated house at the corner of St Anne's Crescent was bought by public subscription for a Pest House where people with serious infectious diseases such as smallpox could be isolated. As the town spread outwards, the Pest

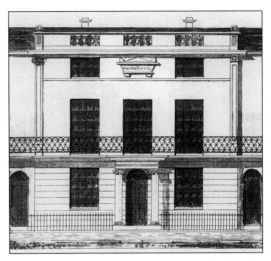

150 Dr. Mantell's Museum, Lewes, sketch of his home, Castle Place, in the garden of which he carried out his excavation.

House was no longer isolated and was therefore sold to St Anne's Parish in 1808 for £450 to be used as a poor house, though the transfer was later found illegal. Other facilities were provided and the Hospital for Infectious Diseases was built in 1876 on Nevill Road. It cost £2,000 and had 19 beds. The medical officer in 1915 was Dr. J.R. Steinhaeuser, who qualified in London and was also on the staff down the road at what was then called the Lewes Victoria Hospital and Dispensary.

The money from the sale of the Pest House went eventually towards providing Lewes with a Public Dispensary which began in July 1847 with four beds in rented premises at 93 High Street. Soon more money was released from the Pest House Charity and the Dispensary moved to 11 High Street, where Benjamin Morris had his house and shop. This opened in 1854 and ten years later became known as the Lewes Dispensary and Infirmary, with a resident medical officer, Dr. Crockford, who ironically had to resign after 11 years on grounds of ill health, as did the first Matron.

In 1886 the *St James's Gazette* wrote admiringly: 'There are, I believe, only two other towns in England which return a lower death-rate than Lewes' but the facilities were beginning to show the strain. In 1887 more space was needed, 16 beds and four cots being thought necessary. As

151 Lewes Dispensary at the foot of School Hill, photographed by Bartlett. In the background is Browne & Crosskey's furniture shop on the corner of Friars Walk.

152 Victoria Hospital in its fine position overlooking the allotments, photograph by Bartlett.

153 Memorial to Mark Sharp, 1747, showing his carpentry tools, in the churchyard of St John sub Castro, photographed by E.A. Meyer.

the year celebrated Queen Victoria's Golden Jubilee, it was decided to christen this the Victoria Hospital. A writer in 1893 said: 'A very excellent work is bring carried on in connection with the hospital, which has large and efficient medical and surgical staffs'.

Despite further improvements, the High Street building began to show signs of being time-expired and the choice of a new site was helped by the willingness of Lord Abergavenny to sell a piece of land at the top of the town. This was done and the new foundation stone was laid by the Duchess of Albany on 9 June 1909. Her husband's aunt, Princess Henry of Battenberg, came to Nevill Road on 2 February 1910 to open the smart new building, completed by Longley & Co. of Crawley, with its 16 beds and four cots. This was the start of the Victoria Hospital which still functions in Lewes, as part of the National Health Service since 1948. The Dispensary which it superseded closed in 1911 and the building catered for a rather different human need, as it became a building society and then a bank. Another Lewes Dispensary operated for 18 years at 51 St Nicholas Lane, but it disappeared from the records in 1930.

If all else failed, then there were two cemeteries in the town. They were the All Saints & Cliffe Cemetery and the St Michael's Cemetery at Rotten Row. In 1915 both were under the care of M.S. Blaker, the clerk to the Burial Board and registrar at 211 High Street. There were also graveyards round most of the churches and non-conformist burial grounds. Many of the memorials are eye-catching or fascinating, like the memorial to Mark Sharp, 1747, showing his carpentry tools, in the churchyard of St John sub Castro. The simplest are those surrounding the Friends Meeting House where the names are recorded, but no elaborate epitaphs.

Ten

Recreation in Lewes

Mark Antony Lower wrote in 1846: 'The inhabitants of Lewes are too commercial in their character (and—shall we say—too intellectual in their pursuits?) to need the excitements of public amusements'. In support of this, he cited the fact that 'the Theatre, which occupied the site of the Mechanics Institution, was never well supported, and has long been abandoned'. He did find some forms of relaxation, starting with the races, and going on to cricket which was said to be the favourite sport, with the bowling green mentioned next, 'to which non-subscribers are admitted on payment of one shilling'. In summer, 'fortnightly meetings of the *South-Saxon Archers* takes place at Coneyborough park, three miles from Lewes, and the season usually terminates with a ball at the County-Hall. It is limited to the gentry'.

Despite Lower's dyspepsia, there have always been many public amusements in Lewes, but the gentry have perhaps had more choice. On 21 September 1734 Thomas Pelham wrote to the head of the Pelham family, the Duke of Newcastle, who had huge estates in East Sussex:

> I've given orders for fitting up the Coffee House and Assembly Rooms as soon as possible. Young Dick Verrall … will come in a month's time to fix himself at Lewes, by which time I hope the Coffee House will be fitted up. Mr Court did not at first relish his House being turn'd to the uses we propose, but I think now seems well satisfied and will remove the rest of his shop goods next week. All our friends are mightily pleased with your Grace's disposition of Court's House.

So began Newcastle House which provided a forum for debate much beloved of the 18th century. Verrall's brother Henry took over the coffee shop in 1742 and remained till 1779, presiding 'with an equal share of respectability and profit'.

The Duke of Newcastle probably preferred a day at the races, for which Lewes was famous. On 12 August 1725 he had written to Lord Carlisle: 'We are here at our horse races, in humble imitation of what you are doing at York, but not so vain as to imagine we can ever come near the perfection you are at'. To the approval of his peers, Newcastle brought to Lewes the method 'which is to give a certificate to the persons that win the plate of their having won it'. Dr. John Burton travelled through Sussex in 1751 and reached Lewes race-course

> in a most well-adapted spot, being moderately sloping and curved. To these races do all the people of the country flock from every quarter, and there is much competition among the fashionable, both the lookers on and those looked at—at night balls for the dancers, and other pleasures. That assemblage indeed is very famous for the number and splendour of the company, and principally because of the high-born Pelhams presiding there, who, as stewards, direct everything in the most sumptuous style.

A famous match took place at Lewes on 27 July 1806 between two celebrated horses, *Sancho*, which belonged to Mr Mellish, and *Pavilion*, which belonged to the Earl of Darlington, for a purse of 2,000 guineas. 'The distance was four miles, equal weight, each horse carrying eight stone seven pounds.' Crowds of over 3,000 assembled from noon onwards and at 1.45pm 'the Prince of Wales arrived upon the ground in his barouche and six beautiful greys', with his friend Sir John Lade who lived in Lewes High Street. *Sancho* was favourite but word got out that it was not well, which proved to be the case.

> Buckle rode *Sancho*, in a white jacket and crimson sleeves. *Pavilion* was ridden by young Chiffney, in a light orange jacket with gold lace stripes. Expectation was now raised to

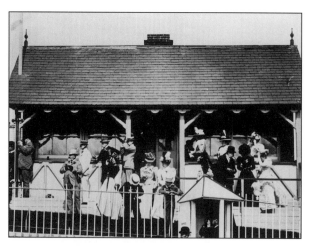

154 King Edward VII, third from left, at Lewes Races, *c*.1905, photograph by Reeves.

155 *Shelley's Hotel.*

its extreme height. The moment of trial at length arrived, and the horses started at ten minutes past two.

When the horses came up to the distance post, 'to the great sorrow and disappointment of everyone, who did not gain by the event, *Sancho* suddenly broke completely down'. His near foot had failed and *Pavilion* ran home and won easily. The Prince and his party, plus Mr. Mellish and his party, adjourned to the *Star Inn*, 'where they alighted, and partook of some refreshment; and at half-past three they returned to Brighton'. Mellish was reputed to have lost £20,000 on the race.

Later travellers may have consulted the *New and Improved Itinerary* for Brighton in 1827 and read:

> The Race-Course, which is about a mile from the town, and on an elevated portion of the Downs, is justly regarded as one of the finest in England. A commodious stand, commanding a view of nearly the whole course, was erected by subscription in the year 1772. The races are held at the close of July or the beginning of August, and continue three days. The king's plate of one hundred guineas, is run for on the first day. The Lewes races formerly possessed sufficient attraction to draw together the lovers of the turf, from every part of the south, and the presence of His Majesty, then Prince of Wales, (who took up his abode in the town, in the house of T. Johnson, Esq. during the

three days) collected together the greater part of the nobility of the district; but these races, like many others, have much fallen off of late years.

His Majesty was better known to racegoers as the Prince Regent and on 8 August 1802 he wrote to his mother: 'Our Races are just concluded last night, & I have been tolerably successful, but a good deal fagg'd by the whole week'.

The 1772 stand was burned down by the military 70 years later, to be replaced by a new one in 1874, enlarged in 1893, and leased to Verrall & Co. Improvements were made to the stands and course in 1860 and in that year the judges had the nightmare scenario of five horses passing the winning post in a dead heat. By 1893 there were meetings there in June, August and November 'and the town is *en fête* during the meetings, which are attended by sportsmen from all parts of the country. All the hotels are then full, and High Street takes on, for the time, the appearance of a fair'. In December 1930 the Lewes Racecourse Co was formed and the meetings attracted a diverse crowd. Virginia Woolf commented on 5 August 1932:

> And now we have been to Lewes races & seen the fat lady in black with parts of her person spilling over the shooting seat on which her bulk is so insecurely poised: seen the riff raff of sporting society all lined up in their cars with the dickies bulging with picnic baskets: heard the bark of bookies; &

seen for a second the pounding straining horses with red faced jockeys lashing them pound by. What a noise they made—what a sense of muscle hard and stretched—& beyond the downs this windy sunny day looked wild & remote; & I could rethink them into uncultivated land again.

The last race meeting took place on 14 September 1964, when the Racecourse was closed against the wishes of the Management, as the Racecourse Levy Board felt that modern racegoers needed more comfort. It was privately sold in 1971 and part of the grandstand was offered for sale in *Country Life* in 1991 for £235,000. Tucked in behind the prison are some new houses on the suitably named new road, The Gallops.

The town's setting among the Downs provides the greatest recreation of all around Lewes, with wonderful views and walks. William Morris wrote: 'You can see Lewes lying like a box of toys under a great amphitheatre of chalk hills … on the whole it is set down better than any town I have seen in England'. Discovering favourite walks is not without its hazards: Gilbert White wrote of Caburn on 30 September 1792:

On the very summit of this exalted promontory, & amidst the trenches of its Danish camp, there haunts a species of wild Bee, making its nest in the chalky soil. When people approach the place, these insects begin to be alarmed, & with a sharp and hostile sound dash and strike round the heads and faces of intruders. I have often been interrupted myself while contemplating the grandeur of the scenery around me, & have thought myself in danger of being stung.

Walkers and others can refresh themselves at a range of inns in Lewes, many of which are long established. Thomas Turner was a frequent visitor, recording details meticulously, such as: 'Mr. French and I dined at *The White Hart* on a piece of boiled beef and greens, a breast of veal roasted and a butter pudding cake'. He often went to an inn at 165-167 High Street, where 'after dinner I went to *The White Horse* where I smoked one pipe with Mr. Fletcher and drank one pint of wine'. Occasionally he went further, as on 4 May 1757: 'We breakfasted at Mr. Thomas Scrase's and dined at Mr. Roase's on 2 pikes roasted and some veal cutlets … We came home about 7 o'clock, but

not sober. Now I am resolved never more to exceed the bounds of moderation'.

Inns were not always built as such and can change their function at any time. *Shelley's* is a good example as it began as the *Vine* and was involved in a legal dispute in 1526. The Shelley family used it as their town house from 1663. One visitor was Dr. Johnson who is said to have become bored with the company of a young Miss Shelley and put her in a cherry tree where she remained for hours until the great lexicographer remembered to tell the family where she was. *Shelley's* became a hotel again in 1932 and now provides a luxurious environment for its guests who have included Arthur Miller and Marilyn Monroe.

Strict licensing laws have to be observed and are sometimes checked. In 1813 John Holman as Constable recorded that he had 'visited Public Houses, all in good order, except the *Lewes Arms* again 2d Time, several persons, in both Parlour, and Tap room Tipling, at ½ past Eleven o Clock, Time of divine Service—gave the Landlord a caution'. Cobbett commented in 1822: 'The inns are good at Lewes, the people civil and not servile, and the charges really (considering the taxes) far below what one could reasonably expect'.

Stanley Baldwin corroborated this much later, referring to the *White Hart* which he said: 'To those whom it may interest you get the best of ale there'. This lovely old building is now a thriving hotel but originally a private house, belonging to the Parker family in the mid-16th century and then the Pelhams of Laughton. From about 1717, its first Master, Richard Verrall, converted it into a fine inn, giving it the name of the defunct *White Hart*, a 17th-century inn at 173 High Street. He died a reasonably wealthy man in 1737, partly thanks to the Club Room which saw weekly Wednesday meetings of a club subsidised by the Duke of Newcastle, who served as Prime Minister and used the *White Hart* as his campaign headquarters.

Richard's son William Verrall took over the *White Hart* when he was only 22, with a background in French cuisine. His name survives because of his book, *A Complete System of Cookery*, in which in 1759 he set out 'a variety of genuine RECEIPTS collected from several Years Experience under the celebrated Mr. de St. Clouet, sometime since Cook to his Grace the Duke of *Newcastle*'. William tried to extend his business, carrying letters between Lewes and

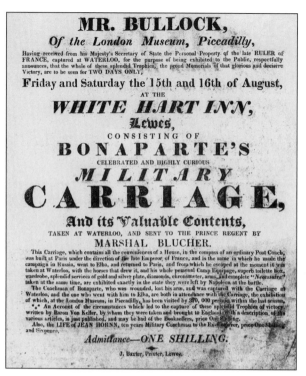

156 Poster advertising the display of Napoleon's Carriage on 15-16 August 1817.

A

COMPLETE SYSTEM

OF

COOKERY.

In which is set forth,

A Variety of genuine RECEIPTS, collected from several Years Experience under the celebrated Mr. de St.Clouet, sometime since Cook to his Grace the Duke of Newcastle.

By WILLIAM VERRAL,
Master of the White-Hart Inn in Lewes, Sussex.

Together with an INTRODUCTORY PREFACE,

Shewing how every Dish is brought to Table, and in what Manner the meanest Capacity shall never err in doing what his Bill of Fare contains.

To which is added,

A true Character of Monsf. de St. Clouet.

LONDON,
Printed for the AUTHOR, and sold by him; As also by EDWARD VERRAL Bookseller, in Lewes: And by John Rivington in St. Paul's Church-yard, London.

M DCC LIX.

157 Title page of William Verrall's cookery book.

Eastbourne and providing stabling for 100 horses, while his brother George held auctions at the *White Hart* and the magistrates used the Great Room for quarter sessions while the Sessions House was rebuilt, but he failed. He was declared bankrupt in March 1761 and died later that month.

Verrall was followed by Thomas Scrase who 'fitted the inn in so commodious a manner as to entertain any personage that shall be pleased to favour him'. He remained until 1791 and soon benefited from the trade brought by the new stage coach, the 'Lewes and Brighton New Flying Machine' which started on 1 November 1761, doing the journey to London in a day. The Headstrong Club started up in Scrase's time, too, and their meetings must have helped the inn's profits. The High Constable usually held his annual dinner there and in 1798 the menu 'consisted of every delicacy of the season', including fresh and potted wheatears.

The *White Hart* continued to make its contribution to Lewes life and occasionally on a wider canvas. An agreement between Arthur Henderson,

the Foreign Secretary, and the Soviet envoy, Mr. Dovgalevsky, was reached on 1 October 1929 to resume diplomatic relations between Britain and Russia. When the House of Commons debated the matter, one speaker blamed Henderson for surrendering to the Soviet demands 'at a hotel where bitter beer is sold and where cricketers are wont to resort'.

Cricket was not closely associated with the *White Hart* but it had been part of leisure in Lewes for many years. A member of the Pelham family had a wager about a cricket match in Lewes in 1694 and an early county game was played here in August 1735. On 19 August 1756 Thomas Turner went to Cliffe Hill to watch a match between

the parish of Mayfield and an eleven pretended to be chosen out of the whole county—but it were only to draw people together. Mayfield went in first and got 78 runs. The pretended county eleven got 55. Then Mayfield went in and got 73, and the county men got about 10 and 3 wickets down, when their time expired.

In June 1775 the Cliffe Hill Cricket Club started and, before rules about boundaries were defined, there were stories of batsmen hitting the ball out of the ground down The Coombe and keeping on running until almost exhausted, before the ball was retrieved. Appropriately there was a *Cricketers Arms* on Chapel Hill to revive players and spectators.

Cricket gradually became more popular. Baxters of Lewes printed an advertisement for a game of cricket on 6 July 1815 between the Gentlemen of Lewes and the Gentlemen of Seaford in Houndean Bottom, Lewes: 'Wickets to be pitched at 10 o'clock precisely. A good Ordinary will be provided on the Ground by the Public's obedient servant, W. Rogers, of the Lamb Inn'. Prizes could be worth while, as on 4 September 1816 when the Gentlemen of the Lewes Club played those of Patcham, Poynings, Pyecombe and Newtimber on Lewes Hill near the Race Stand for 50 guineas. Sadly the results do not survive but the pattern continued, with the addition of the Lewes Priory Cricket Club. This club, whose ground, according to the 1893 *Descriptive Account*, 'known as the Dripping Pan, is the finest in the County, is one of the best clubs in the South of England: and was a well-known training school for the County Eleven - now, alas, fallen upon evil days', over 100 years ago! Kelly's *Directory* records that the Dripping Pan, 'together with Mountfield House, the Mount and the Convent Garden, containing in all upwards of 10 acres, was presented to the Corporation in 1895 by Aubrey Hillman esq. J. P.'.

There are public grass and hard tennis courts nearby, plus the Southdown Tennis Club whose excellent facilities have helped the talented British player, Clare Wood. Swimming at the Pells has already been mentioned, as has the unique Bowling Green, though bowling also takes place near the Priory Mound and in the Grange gardens. Sporting enthusiasts in Lewes have also had access to facilities for football, rugby, cycling, rowing, angling, quoiting, rifle shooting and whippet racing, not to mention the Sussex speciality of stoolball. There was also golf which was played on Cliffe Hill from 1893. The first Secretary, Ronald Morris, noted in 1896 that

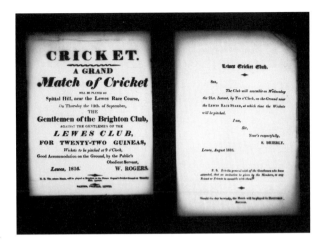

158 Cricket poster of 1816.

through the kindness of Mr Wallis (the tenant farmer of Cliffe Hill) several gentlemen have been enabled to initiate themselves into the mysteries of the Royal and Ancient game for the last three years and to develop their enthusiasm by playing over a natural unmade course on Cliffe Hill.

From 1887 there was a boom in golf course building in Sussex and Lewes formalised its Golf Club in the magnificent setting on top of Cliffe Hill in 1896.

Lewes has an active artistic life, too, with talented individuals too numerous to mention, though ranging from the script writer for *Spiceworld the Movie* to the artist commissioned to create a sculptural reed bed as a millennium project on the Railway Land, now a local nature reserve. A new gallery is planned for the Town Hall, adding to the private facilities already available to artists and craftsmen, amateur and professional, building on the work of the Ladies of Millers and others. Jane Austen is said to have attended a function at the Town Hall, when it was the *Star*. The novelist Jeffrey Farnol had a special place by the bar in the *White Hart* in the 1930s and Daisy Ashford wrote *The Young Visiters* at the age of nine in 1890, whilst living at Southdown House. Much nearer our own time, the writer, illustrator and stamp designer, C. Walter Hodges, came to live in Southover and designed the Shakespeare theatre stamps. Members of the Bloomsbury Group visited Lewes regularly from nearby Rodmell or Charleston and Virginia Woolf briefly had property in Lewes. New writers have been helped

159   Cricket at the Dripping Pan, photograph by Reeves.

latterly by schemes such as the Asham Award for short stories by women writers which attracted over 900 entries in 1998.

There has long been an active interest in music in Lewes and Lower noted in 1846 that 'a *Quintette Society* has been established, and public concerts are occasionally given at the Hall'. Nearby Glyndebourne makes its impact locally and nationally in the summer and on the railway time-table all year round, with one evening train chang-ing the timing of the regular stop at Lewes to assist those returning from the opera to London. The regular performances by the Lewes Amateur Dramatic Society are well attended, as are con-certs of a range of music indoors or in the open air. The annual ARTwave festival opens at the end of August with jazz and samba at the Castle, while music has always been a part of Bonfire Night with marching bands in the procession. Charles Wille's diary for 6 November 1848 re-corded 'the usual festival held on the Wallands, faggots, beer & band being given by gentlemen to keep the fireworks out of the Town'. Now the active Nicholas Yonge Society keeps alive the name of the Lewes-born musician who intro-duced and popularised Italian madrigals into

England, publishing *Musica Transalpina* in 1588. He is to be commemorated by a bronze sculp-ture of two singing figures by Austin Bennett, installed in the Grange Gardens as a millennium project.

Drama too flourishes in Lewes. There was a temporary theatre in Lewes in 1770 and a new one built by Mr. Fox in 1789 with 10 subscribers who were asked to pay £50 each in return for free tickets for 21 years. The first performance was on 10 August 1789. Mr. Fox had a good business eye, as in November 1789 an advertise-ment appeared:

> To be let, two convenient dwelling-houses, one on each side of the Theatre, very eligible for the sale of fruit and other refreshments to the audience, there being doors of communication from the parlour of each to the Theatre. They are within the Borough of Lewes. Apply Mr Fox, Manager, etc.

This was at the top of St John Street, later Police Barracks.

This theatre and others did not survive but Lewes now boasts the Lewes Little Theatre. The Lewes Players belonged to an amateur society formed in 1929, which became one of the best amateur groups in the South and won first place in the 1936 British Drama League Festival with *Libel*. Their base was St Michael's Church Hall on Watergate Lane, formerly known as the County Theatre, but in 1936 East Sussex County Council bought it for an extension to Pelham House. The Lewes Players therefore bought the derelict Providence Chapel in Lancaster Street for £400, thanks to a mortgage and donations from many local people, including John Maynard Keynes and two MPs. Spearheaded by the Rev. Kenneth Rawlings and Victor Brown, the treasurer for 20 years, they decided to convert the chapel into a theatre themselves and run it as the Lewes Theatre Club with a membership of 100. They aimed to open in 1939 but the war intervened. The first production, of A.P. Herbert's *Double Demon* and Philip Johnson's *Today of all Days*, was staged on November 1940. In 1949 a limited company was formed under the title of Lewes Little Theatre Ltd. who refurbished the theatre and expanded the facilities. The theatre held 130 and there were 500 members. In 1992 the company was wound up and its assets and functions transferred to Lewes Theatre Club which continues to provide an interesting range of productions each year to its membership.

F. Frankfort Moore reported in the 1920s: "The last indignity offered to a part of St Mary in Foro was to remove the stone work and the fine old door of the porch in order to adapt the remainder to the requirements of one of the two cinemas in the town'. In common with many other towns, neither has survived but film buffs can go to the regular meetings of the Lewes Film Club at All Saints or else to Brighton, before the cinemas there also succumb to competition from sophisticated home entertainment. Styles change and the leisure industry responds to needs, with a new Leisure Centre and Arts Centres taking over buildings that started out catering for very different tastes. The Borough Museum has now gone but visitors can still go to Barbican House and Anne of Cleves House, run by the Sussex Archaeological Society. Esther Meynell, writing in 1936, encouraged everyone to share her enthusiasm for Barbican House and for her favourite exhibits there, in particular

160 Drawing by C. Walter Hodges for a commemorative cover at Anne of Cleves House to accompany the stamps of the Six Wives of Henry VIII, 21 January 1997.

the skeleton of the early Bronze Age young woman found at the Trundle, sleeping an enchanted sleep in her glass case in the attitude in which she was found—she looks so young still, after all these thousands of years, getting on for something like, 4,000— her bones are so small and slender, one can imagine her running with a light-foot grace.

Such images remain and help to fill our modern leisure with more than the electronic wizardry of computer games and DVD.

Eleven

The Coming of the Railways

Railways revolutionised the way that people travelled and thought about travelling. Not everyone approved: Ruskin complained that by providing a rail link in Derbyshire, 'now every fool in Buxton can be in Bakewell in half-an-hour, and every fool in Bakewell at Buxton'. Sensible people also needed to travel and the transport network gradually expanded to fit in with their needs. It could be risky, as Blaker remembered that 'Mr. Lutley, who had a good deal to do with the construction of the line, told me he had more than once driven up Falmer Hill sitting on the safety valve of his engine'.

In 1836 Wille recorded in his diary a meeting 'at the *Star Inn* respecting the rail road from London to Brighton'. The original Act of Parliament of 15 July 1837 authorised the link between Brighton, Lewes and Newhaven, but funds ran out before it could be built. The Brighton, Lewes and Hastings Railway Company stepped into the breach, with John Rastrick as their engineer. A new Act of 29 July 1844 allowed them initially to make the line from Brighton to St Leonards, with provision for double track to Lewes. Section 328 of the Act gave the company specific power to sell the undertaking to the London & Brighton Railway, and this was done in August 1845, at a cost of £35,000. The route was difficult as a curved viaduct was needed over the old turnpike road at the Brighton end. A smaller viaduct nearer Lewes at Hodshrove performed the same function and the *Lewes Guide* of 1846 commented that it 'affords a striking specimen of modern improvement in the building of arches'.

Between this viaduct and Lewes stood a different obstruction, the ruins of the Priory of St Pancras. As part of the site was much higher than the line, a cutting 40 feet wide by 12 feet deep was needed. This went smoothly until on

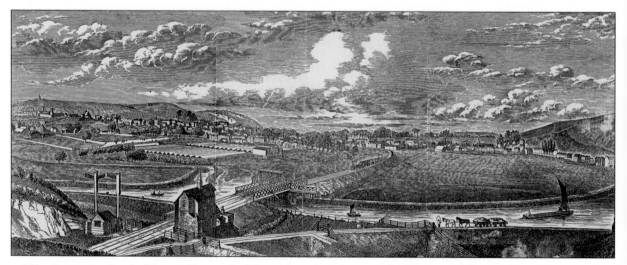

161 Panoramic view by Thomas Henwood of Lewes from the Prison and the Priory to Cliffe, showing a wide range of transport, from a horse-drawn cart to a train.

162 Discovery of the remains of Gundrada and William de Warenne at the Lewes Priory, October 1845, from a drawing by W.E. Baxter. It shows the cutting with the workers to the left and the top-hatted antiquarians and their wives to the right, guarding the cists.

28 October 1845 a workman 'pushed his shovel against something which was first supposed to be a stone slab'. The local antiquarians watching this area they must have been surprised at their good fortune when the supposed stone slab turned out to be the lead box or cist containing the bones of Gundrada, soon to be followed by that of her husband, William de Warenne, the Norman founders of the Priory. A kind fate had even preserved their Christian names on the lids, to remove all doubt of the importance of this find, which was taken up by the national press.

The directors of the railway gave every facility for the careful removal of relics. Other finds were made and the site attracted sight-seers: Dr. Gideon Mantell wrote in his Journal for 6 December that, after walking to the Priory to see the railway cutting, he 'went to the Church to see the coffins. Several skeletons were found, and fragments of encaustic tiles, but few with good figures, and none so interesting as those I dug up some 25 years ago'. The article on the finds for the British Archaeological Association commented: 'It almost requires the iron conscience of a railway to be proof against the curses denounced in his charter by William de Warenne on any who should disturb his foundation'.

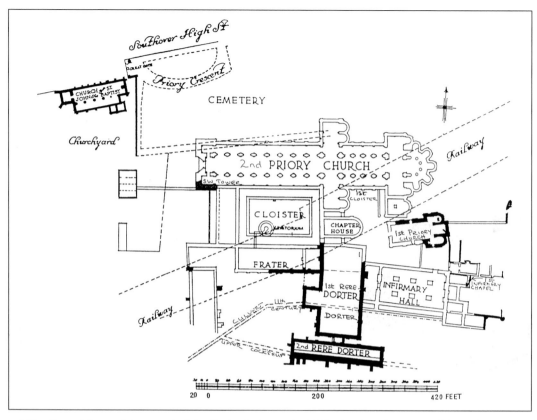

163 Plan of Lewes Priory, revised by Freda Anderson in 1995, showing the route of the railway line through the most important part of the Priory, its Great Church and Chapter House.

164 The railway line and Lewes Priory, photographed by Meads in the 1920s.

The discoveries at the Priory led directly to the foundation in 1846 of the Sussex Archaeological Society, 'at the suggestion of a few gentlemen in the town and neighbourhood of Lewes'. It had a membership of 90, including Lower, Mantell and other like-minded enthusiasts, with a common aim to 'promote a readier acquaintance among persons attached to the same pursuits, and to combine their exertions in illustration of the History and Antiquities of Sussex'. Others set up a fund to build a chapel to house the founders' remains in the church of St John the Baptist nearby. The directors of the railway company contributed £50 to this fund, though Lower suggested cynically that this was 'with a business eye, to create a new Lion for the fashionable loungers of Brighton—an excuse for their coming to Lewes'. Whatever the reason, the chapel was completed in 1847.

Writing his *Handbook for Lewes* just before the line opened, Lower thought that from a commercial point of view

> no event in the annals of Lewes is so important as the passing of the Act for the formation of the Brighton, Lewes, and Hastings Railway. A few months will bring this great public work to its completion, thus placing Lewes within a two hours' ride of the metropolis. ... forming as it does a large part of the great coast line, it will be a considerable national advantage.

Despite problems with the bridges on the route, the line to Lewes opened on 8 June 1846 and the length to St Leonards (West Marina) was opened later that year. It was immediately popular and some 1,800 passengers travelled between Lewes and Brighton on the first Sunday after it opened. Lower heard that the works from Brighton to St Leonards were to cost a little more than £500,000, 'and the undertaking promises a very satisfactory return to the projectors'. The link between Hastings and Lewes was finished on 13 February 1851.

Charles Wille, too, was monitoring the railway's progress in his diary. On 29 November 1845, he wrote that James Senior was 'kill'd at Southeram by railway waggons'. On 6 April 1848 he noted: 'The Engine ran on the line from Southram to Kingstone for the 1st Time.' On 3 June 'Col. Paizley inspected the line from Brighton to Lewes' and after the Lewes line opened on 8 June, he recorded on 27 June: 'Hastings Railway opened, four trains each way.' Later that first year, on 10

September, 'the luggage train from Hastings ran down an incline to the brook, went over the bank and the engine fell into Spring Ditch. No lives lost', though it took two days to recover the engine, 'after much labour'.

Mantell travelled from London to Lewes on 29 June 1846, noting in his Journal that he

> started by the 9 o'clock train for Brighton—a beautiful day—reached the terminus at half past eleven. Started at twelve by the Lewes railway which has but lately been opened, and is now in an unfinished state. About 15 minutes and we arrived at Lewes, at the site of the Friars which has been entirely demolished and all traces swept away.

Mantell had published an account of William IV's visit to the Friars and his welcome by Nehemiah Wimble, so he knew the area in its pre-railway days. The next day, after staying with a friend at Barcombe, he

> left at ten in an open phaeton, by Cook's bridge to see the cuttings forming in the chalk marl by the railway now constructing from Keymer by Lewes to Newhaven. Returned with my brother to the Hamsey road to obtain some fossils from the 'Navies' as the railway labourers are now termed. Some good turrilites—one fragment the largest but one I ever saw—Ammonites, etc. two fine Mantili etc.

He then returned to Lewes with his cargo of fossils and caught the train back to Brighton and on to London.

This trip encouraged him to urge the readers of his next publication, *A Day's Ramble in and about the Ancient Town of Lewes*, to 'purchase one of the excellent "*Railway Chronicle* Travelling Charts" and do the Brighton to Lewes journey which is generally passed over in fifteen minutes'. He was surprised by the last stages of the route into Lewes:

> This sudden divergence of the Railway from what appears to be the direct line to the heart of the town, namely, along the valley, to the bottom of St Mary's Street, has doubtless been found necessary from the existence of insurmountable engineering difficulties, which the common observer will in vain seek to discover.

Despite the new station's distance from the town centre, there were 'always vehicles of various kinds

165 Lewes railway track, without sleepers, from a glass negative.

in waiting for the arrival of the trains, and carriages of every description may be hired for excursions to distant places'.

The station that Mantell described was at Friars Walk. The week before it opened, the *Sussex Advertiser* announced: 'The temporary booking office and waiting room erected at the Friars Station is now completed and presents a very neat appearance'. This temporary wooden booking office was replaced by a permanent one on 29 August that year, but the roofing was not completed until February 1848. The station survived into the 1960s, a five-bay building of yellow brick in the classical style, and the contemporary *Railway Times* said that 'Mr. Rastrick is the Engineer-in-Chief and Mr. Fabian of Brighton is the Contractor for the permanent station at Lewes'.

The same issue of the paper commented on another station closer to Brighton and known as

Ham or Southover Station:

> Last week the ground was excavated for the foundations of the station to be erected at the bottom of St Mary's Lane; or rather at the bottom of the new road made from Lansdown Terrace. It is to be immediately opposite the temporary blacksmith's shop there, but on the All Saints side of the railroad, and intended for the accommodation of the inhabitants of Southover. It will be of very small dimensions.

There were also up and down platforms at Pinwell, just east of Friars Walk, which was in use about 1847. As these and the later stations were always known as Lewes, these through platforms were presumably considered as part of one station.

The route from London into Lewes was surveyed by John Urpeth Rastrick in 1844 and included a stretch of tunnel 397 yards long, just

166   An early view of the later railway station, from a glass negative.

before Lewes Station. There can be no more appropriate place to look at the plan for this than the East Sussex Record Office, on the direct line, where the accompanying Book of Reference details the land ownership in the section described as the Precincts of the Castle of Lewes. It began with John Langford's Brewery and then went under the Bowling Green, which was owned by the then Earl of Abergavenny. This descendant of the medieval Nevilles was one of the Lords of the Borough of Lewes, along with the Duke of Norfolk and the Earl de la Warr, who were the owners of a patch of rough land and waste land on the line of the new route, plus part of the Castle Wall and Castle Gateway, then occupied by the South Saxon Lodge of Freemasons, whose Secretary was Richard Butcher. The Turnpike Road from Lewes to Offham and Witch Cross was listed, belonging to the Trustees of such Road, with Francis Harding Gill their clerk. The Commissioners of the Borough of Lewes and their clerk, William Polhill Kerr, were also mentioned as owners of the public roads under which the track went, at Watergate Lane, St Martin's Lane, Back Lane and High Street.

Lewes achieved its direct link to London as a result of the navvies' work that Mantell had witnessed. A line from Keymer Junction linking

up with the Brighton-Hastings line at Lewes was authorised on 30 June 1845. Licences 'to construct maintain and use a Tunnel' were granted in December 1846 and the line opened to the public on 1 October 1847, though freight services had begun earlier. Again Wille was on hand to record the first day, when he 'went to London and back. Keymer line open'd, went by Lewes train to 3 Bridges—back by Brighton'. Next, 'a railway line leads south to the sea, through the marshy lands called Lewes Levels'. This was the Newhaven and Seaford branch, authorised on 18 June 1846. The Newhaven section opened at the end of the following year, for freight first and then passengers, but the Seaford link had to wait for the powers to be revived in 1862.

The coming of the railway was not universally acclaimed. The Rev. Edward Boys Ellman recollected:

Before there was a railroad there were in Lewes two large wholesale grocers' firms, which supplied the various country shops for many miles around. When the railroads were opened the country shops obtained their stores much more largely from London. The gentry also, and especially the ladies, instead of making their purchases at Lewes, went by train to Brighton, which was vastly increasing

167   The town's second railway station, built in 1857, photographed by Reeves.

168   The top of Station Street where it meets High Street. The sign on the shop to the left points people down towards the railway station.

in size and in importance. The consequence was that the trade of Lewes went down, and the shops gave up keeping goods for which there was no demand.

It was all change at Lewes Station on 1 November 1857 when the Friars Walk station closed, though it remained in use for goods traffic, and the new one opened in the Ham Fields, built by Henry Davey of Lewes and Mr. Fabian of Brighton. The street bringing road traffic to the new station was extended and renamed Station Street, rather that St Mary's Lane from the church of St Mary in Foro. The Chairman of the London, Brighton and South Coast Railway assured his shareholders that year that the old station 'was the most incomplete and injudicious station ever erected; but we have now provided not only for our present, but for all the future requirements at that spot'.

A new line was opened on 11 October 1858 for the Lewes & Uckfield Railway Company, an independent local company, who had been authorised to build the straightforward Lewes and Uckfield line in the Act of 27 July 1857. This

169   The train kept going, before the days of the third rail, no matter what the conditions were like. Here the wrong sort of water on the line of Lewes Brooks at Landport did not prevent the train from coming in from Offham, where the church can be seen in the distance on the left. Photograph by Bartlett.

would join together an important agricultural centre with the county town and the expected increase in traffic was the final argument in persuading the LBSCR, who bought this line in 1859, to create a new Lewes station in the fork of the Brighton and Keymer lines in 1857.

A line from Lewes to Tunbridge Wells had been suggested in 1844 but final agreement to a new company, the Brighton, Uckfield and Tunbridge Wells Railway, had to wait for 20 years. The LBSCR built a new section of line, known as the Hamsey Deviation, involving a new 3½-mile stretch of track from Hamsey into the north end of Lewes Station, which meant that trains going to Uckfield no longer left Lewes via the tunnel. The new line opened on 3 August

1868. The *Sussex Advertiser* of 30 September announced that from 1 October, 'the trains from Lewes to Tunbridge Wells, instead of starting on the London line and branching off at the present Uckfield Junction, will proceed by way of the newly-constructed line commencing at the end of the Brighton platform and passing over the bridge near the Fitzroy Library'. This new stretch of line rose gradually on a viaduct which passed over the site of the original station: of ten original brick arches, its, four went when the line was improved in 1889.

There were occasional serious accidents. Wille recorded one on 6 June 1851, 'an accident on the Brighton & Lewes rail. 4 kill'd, one very much hurt'. Another accident happened

170 Fitzroy House and the railway bridge, looking east, photographed by Reeves.

171   Accident at Lewes Station, 27 September 1879, photographed by Reeves.

about 9.30 on 18 October 1854 near Pin Well when the unfortunate victim as said to have been 'cut to Pieces'. On 27 September 1879, a Hastings-London passenger train stopped at Lewes station

and took water while the driver went round with his oil can. As Driver Rookwood received the 'right-away' and eased forward, the firebox blew up, showering the train and station with steam, boiling water, soot, coal and ballast. The engine was thrown off the rails, its smokebox door blown off, and Rookwood was found dead on the roof of the second carriage. His fireman and guard were injured but survived.

The engine was examined and it transpired that the safety valves had been tampered with and set to blow off at 140 per square inch instead of the usual 120 setting.

In 1877 the Lewes & East Grinstead Railway was authorised, with a branch from Horsted Keynes to Haywards Heath, and opened in 1882. As some of the lines through Lewes had severe curvature, an Act was passed on 3 July 1884 to deviate and remodel the lines around the station where necessary. As part of this exercise, the 1857 station was entirely rebuilt on a site slightly south-east of the earlier site. The changeover came on 17 June 1889 and this third station is the one with which modern commuters are familiar, though the old carriage canopy has gone the way of the horse-drawn vehicles that it once protected. The whole station saw extensive changes in 1999, not least the new barriers.

There was a social side for the workforce. In 1890, for instance, the annual supper for the men employed at the Lewes Goods Station took place at the *Elephant and Castle Inn*. John Stone, the

172 The new Lewes Railway Station, opened in 1889, with its carriage canopy, photographed by Reeves.

THE COMING OF THE RAILWAYS

173   Station Street at the junction of Southover Road and Lansdowne Place. Opposite the *Lansdowne*, which still exists, is the *New Station Inn* which was demolished in 1963.

Goods Superintendent, presided over an assembly of over 30 people. After the supper, the guests were informed that the shareholders of the LBSCR had had a prosperous year. Various improvements were then suggested, in particular the need to devise some means 'whereby the customers of the Company could be saved a tramp through the "oceans of mud" which now covered the yard'. The evening ended with singing and 'thanks to the kindness of the Magistrates, the harmony was prolonged until midnight'.

The 1921 Railways Act brought into being the Southern Railway, the smallest of the new companies, on 1 January 1923. It was created by merging other companies in the south-east with the London Brighton & South Coast who had covered the triangle of land from London to Hastings and Portsmouth, with a monopoly in

central Sussex. Under Sir Herbert Walker as general manager, it became the biggest electrified suburban system owned by any one railway in the world and one of the most involved in rail-sea links. The Southern absorbed the long established Newhaven Harbour Company in 1926, keeping the important cross-Channel links going.

Work was done on the station in 1934-5, prior to electrification. The platforms were lengthened, a new signal box was built, the Southover Road bridge was reconstructed and the tunnel entrance was widened. British Rail took over from Southern Railway on 1 January 1948. On 6 January 1969 the Uckfield to Lewes line closed, despite howls of protest from rail users. South East Traffic commissioners received applications for road licences for additional buses to fill the gap. In recent years,

the rail network at Lewes has been part of
Network South East and latterly Connex, the
French company.

Changes happened to the nearby roads, too.
In 1883 an amendment was lost

> that the Surveyor be directed to pave kerb
> and channel the east side of Station Street
> from the South corner of the Wesleyan
> Chapel to the bottom at an estimated cost of
> £28 18s. 9d. for material, the Corporation
> workmen to execute the work.

Opposite the *Lansdowne Arms* stood the *New
Station Inn*, built to cater for those using the new
station. It was demolished in 1963 to improve
visibility for traffic, but it remains a road crossing
to be undertaken with great caution.

Commuters now form one sector of the
Lewes population, alongside the original core of
families who have lived and worked here for
generations. The arrival of the University of Sussex
at Falmer in 1962 brought new residents to Lewes,
as did Brighton Polytechnic which is now also a
University. It remains to be seen whether Lewes
absorbs all these new factors in the same way that
it has since the locals banded together against a
Viking threat, but the result will be just one more
element in the kaleidoscope that is Lewes. The
town straddles the meridian from Landport
through the *Black Horse Hotel* on Western Road,
so time is its ally. In return it has used time well,
interweaving the old and new, largely successfully, and should continue to do so for the next
thousand years.

History repeats itself and the wheel can come
full circle. *The Guardian* of 26 March 2000
produced a list of the two hundred richest people
in Britain since 1066. Lewes today accommodates
varying degrees of wealth, including a major lot-
tery winner but, allowing for problems in
translating 11th century incomes accurately into
modern terms, the wealthiest man in this list was
William de Warenne whose lands and estates were
valued at £57 billion. In 1066, therefore, Lewes
had a licence to print money and rapidly became
a much loved part of the holdings of an immensely
rich man, whose earthly remains are still in the
town. Assuming that the passion for making lists
survives for a further millennium, another
individual may top the ratings, but the true wealth
of Lewes will be there in the setting of this jewel
in the Downs.

Bibliography

This book, like so many others on Sussex history, depends on the relevant volumes of the *Victoria County History*. The other main sources are the *Sussex Archaeological Collections*, still going strong after 150 years, and the *Sussex Notes and Queries*. There is also the wealth of primary information in the volumes of the Sussex Record Society, the transcripts of documents in the Public Record Office, such as the *Acts of the Privy Council* and the *Calendar* series, and of Coroners' Inquests and Assize Records. Documents, reference works, magazines for churches, chapels and schools, and newspaper cuttings have been consulted in Barbican House Library and Museum, the East and West Sussex Record Offices, Lambeth Palace Library, the Library of the Gospel Standard Baptists, public libraries in Brighton, Lewes, Haywards Heath, Shoreham, Worthing, the University of Sussex and many private individuals. Other sources are as follows:

General

Austen, Brian, Cox, Don and Upton, John (ed.), *Sussex Industrial Archaeology; A Field Guide* (1985)
Bennett, Elizabeth, *My memories of Lewes over the many years* (1997)
Black's Guide to the South-Eastern Counties of England (1861)
Blaker, Nathaniel Paine, *Sussex in Bygone Days* (1919)
Cobbett, William, *Rural Rides*, intro. Asa Briggs (1967)
Curwen, E. Cecil (ed.), *The Journal of Gideon Mantell* (1940)
Davey, L.S., *The Street Names of Lewes* (1961)
A Descriptive Account of Lewes, Seaford, and Newhaven (1893)
Drewett, Peter, *Rescue Archaeology in Sussex, 1976* (1977)
Dudeney, Mrs. H., *A Lewes Diary 1916-1944*, edited by Diana Crook (1998)
Dunvan, P., *Ancient and Modern History of Lewes and Brighthelmston* (1795)
Ellman, Rev. Edward Boys, *Recollections of a Sussex Parson* (1925)
Godfrey, Walter, *Some Lewes Townsfolk of the Past* (1926)
Godfrey, W., *Lewes: The Official Guide to the Historic County Town* (c.1938)
Holman, George, *Some Lewes Men of Note* (1905)
Holman, George, *Some Reminiscences* (1930)
Horsfield, Rev. Thomas Walker, *The History and Antiquities of Lewes* (1824)
Horsfield, T.W., *The History, Antiquities, and Topography of the County of Sussex* (1835)
Kelly's *Directories* etc.
Kitch, Dr. Malcolm (ed.), *Studies in Sussex Church History* (1981)
Lewes Archaeological Group, *Aspects of Archaeology in the Lewes Area* (1987)
Lower, Mark Antony, *A Handbook for Lewes* (c.1846)
Lower, M.A., *A Compendious History of Sussex* (1870)
Lucas, E.V., *Highways and Byways in Sussex* (1904)
Lucas, E.V., *The Old Contemporaries* (1935)

Mantell, Dr. Gideon, *A Day's Ramble in Lewes* (1846)
Pevsner, Nikolaus & Nairn, Ian, *Sussex* (1965/70)
Sawyer, John, *A Guide to Lewes* (1897)
Sussex County Magazine articles
Sussex Genealogist and Local Historian articles
Sussex History articles
Sussex Industrial Archaeology: A Field Guide (1985)
Vaisey, D. (ed.), *The Diary of Thomas Turner 1754-1765* (1984)
Wille, Charles, *Diary of a Lewes Tradesman (1832-1876)*
Woollgar, T., *Spicilegia* (c.1810)

Lewes Landmarks

Allcroft, A. Hadrian, *Downland Pathways* (1922-24)
Savage, Anne (ed.), *Anglo-Saxon Chronicles* (1996)
Carpenter, D., *The Battle of Lewes and the Battle of Evesham* (1987)
Morris, John (ed.), *Domesday Book: Sussex* (1976)
Drewett, P., Rudling, D., Gardiner, M., *The South-East to AD 1000* (1988)
Gibbs, Vicary (ed.), *Complete Peerage*
Glover, Judith, *Sussex Place-Names* (1997)
Jones, D., *Saint Richard of Chichester* (1995)
Lyne, M., *Lewes Priory Excavations by Richard Lewes 1969-82* (1997)
Mason, J.F.A., *William the First and the Sussex Rapes* (1966)
Goring, J., *Sussex and the Spanish Armada* (1988)
Woolf, Virginia, *Congenial Spirits: the Letters of Virginia Woolf* (1989)
Woolf, Virginia, *Diary*, Vol.IV, 1931-35 (1982)

Later Landmarks

Davey, L., *The Inns of Lewes past and present* (1977)
Etherington, J., *Lewes Bonfire Night* (1993)
Hart, B., *The Lewes Lads (A memoir of war-time evacuation)* (1999)

The Incorporation of Lewes: Proclamation of the Charter (1881)

Jenkins, D., May, J., Le Follic, S., Nakov, C. (eds.), *Rodin in Lewes* (1999)

Keane, John, *Tom Paine* (1995)

Pelham House: A Brief History (1979)

Sox, D., *Bachelors of Art: Edward Perry Warren and the Lewes House Brotherhood* (1991)

Thomas-Stamford, Charles, *Sussex in the Great Civil War* (1910)

Title Deed of Settlement of the Lewes Gas-Light Company (1822)

The Works of William Laud (1977)

Lewes and its rivers

An Act for improving the Navigation of the River Ouse (1791)

Barty-King, Hugh, *Sussex in 1839* (1974)

Whitaker, William & Reid, Clement, *The Water Supply of Sussex* (1899)

Universal British Directory (1793)

Lewes and its roads

Brighton, by the Five Great Roads: New and Improved Itinerary (1827)

Defoe, Daniel, *A Tour through England & Wales* [1724-6] (1927)

The Diary of Joseph Farington (1978)

The Diary of Sylas Neville, 1767-1788 (1950)

East Sussex Federation of Women's Institutes, *East Sussex within Living Memory* (1995)

Jenner, C. Underwood, *My Reminiscences* (1924)

Journal of the House of Commons

Lewes Town Centre—the Problems, submission by the Friends of Lewes (July 1970)

Lucas, E.V., *The Old Contemporaries* (1935)

Orchard, S.C. and Smith, W.L.H., *The History of the Post Office* (1992)

Straker, Ernest, *Wealden Iron* (1969)

Sutton, Rev. C.N., *Historical Notes of Withyham* (1902)

Religious Life

Butler, Rev. Alban, *The Lives of the Saints*, Vol. IV, April (1933)

Chamberlain, Jeffery S., *Accommodating High Churchmen* (1997)

Elphick, George, *Sussex Bells and Belfries* (1970)

Mayhew, G.J., 'The Progress of the Reformation in East Sussex 1530-1559', *Southern History*, Vol. V (1983)

Nye, J., *A small account of my travels through the wilderness*, edited by V. Gammon (*c.*1982)

Salter, Walter E. *et al.*, *Some Notes on the History of Lewes Meeting House* (1934)

Stoneham, Edward T., *Sussex Martyrs of the Reformation* (1967)

Wright, Thomas, *The Life of William Huntington* (1909)

Lewes Markets and Fairs

Board of Agriculture reports: *The Agricultural State of the Kingdom* (1816)

Brooks, Ray, *Sussex Flights and Fliers 1783-1919* (1992)

Tuppen, Len, *Only Yesterday: Len Tuppen's life as a shepherd in the 1920s* (1993)

White, Gilbert, *Journals*, edited by Walter Johnson (1970)

Young, Rev. Arthur, *General View of the Agriculture of Sussex* (1813)

Law and Order

Bridges, Brian, Foster, Geoff and Lloyd, David, *Lewes Police Station Centenary 1884-1984* (1984)

Coogan, Tim Pat, *De Valera: Long Fellow, Long Shadow* (1993)

History of Lewes Prison (*c.*1964)

Lewes Police of Yesteryear (*c.*1970s)

Minutes of Evidence before Select Committee on Gaols and Houses of Correction (1835)

Minutes of Evidence taken before the Select Committee on Prison Discipline (1850)

Health

Davey, L.S., *The Story of the Lewes Victoria Hospital* (1981)

Pocock, David, *Pesthouse Field: The Story of St Anne's Crescent, Lewes* (1996)

Recreation

Burstow, G.P., *Early 19th Century Cricket in the Lewes Area* (*c.*1963)

The Game of Bowls at the Tilting Ground, Lewes (1968)

Moore, F Frankfort, *A few hours in Lewes* (*c.*1930)

Verrall, William, *A Complete System of Cookery* (1759)

White, Graham, *The History of Lewes Golf Club 1896-1996* (1995)

Education

Bédoyère, Guy de la, *The Diary of John Evelyn* (1994)

Bradshaw, N.R.J., *Alma Mater* (*c.*1980)

The Chronicle of the County Grammar School for Girls Lewes, 1964

Hibbs, Alan, *Southdown House, Lewes* (1987)

Tibble, Ronald, 'The Pattern of Schooling in Lewes', *Sussex History*, Vol.2, No.2 (Autumn 1981)

School magazines

The railways

Bonavia, Michael R., *The History of the Southern Railway* (1987)

Lee, Charles E., *The Lewes Station Mystery* (1950)

Turner, J.T., Howard, *London Brighton and South Coast Railway*, 3 Volumes (1977-9)

Index

References in **bold** refer to pages on which there are illustrations.